TRASH ANIMALS

The animal weirdos we secretly love

Rachel Federman

Illustrated by Clare Faulkner

Harper Collins

HarperCollins*Publishers*
1 London Bridge Street
London SE1 9GF

WilliamCollinsBooks.com

HarperCollins*Publishers*
Macken House, 39/40 Mayor Street Upper,
Dublin 1, D01 C9W8, Ireland

First published by HarperCollins*Publishers* in 2025

1 3 5 7 9 10 8 6 4 2

Written by Rachel Federman
Front cover and interior illustrations by Clare Faulkner
Design by Jacqui Caulton and e-Digital Design
Publishing Director: Caitlin Doyle
Production Controller: Alan Cracknell
Copyeditor: Helena Caldon
Proofreader: Rachel Malig

A catalogue record for this book is available from the British Library.
Library of Congress Cataloging-in Details have been applied for.

ISBN 978-0-00-876182-0

Printed and bound in Latvia

This book contains FSC™ certified paper and other controlled sources to ensure responsible forest management.

For more information visit: www.harpercollins.co.uk/green

For Mom—Back when the car windows were open on highways in summer, we loved the smell of skunk cabbage together, remember? And what fun we had watching "Joe"—the series of squirrel visitors to the back porch who feasted on our jack-o'-lanterns each November.

CONTENTS

INTRODUCTION

Move over Grumpy Cat and Lil Bub, there's a new mammal in town. Trash animals are making their way into the headlines ... and into our hearts. "Louie the Raccoon" has over half a million followers on Instagram; Gizmo the Skunk, 36,000 and counting. Sure, funny cat videos still make us laugh, but watching zoological outcasts relax on the couch has made us do something equally as valuable—rethink our predispositions against them, and maybe our own place in the Earth's ecosystem as well.

The more we learn about these outside animals, routinely cast out from basements and backyards, the more impressed we are likely to be. A carrier pigeon's flight home to Scotland led to the successful rescue of a downed aircraft in the North Sea during World War II. Snakes have friends. Beavers help combat climate change. Crows may understand the concept of zero. And now, suddenly, instead of shooing them away as pests, many are enjoying watching the

daily lives of these one-time weirdoes. And it's not a few eccentric raccoon fans who have embraced these furry foragers; the underdog, or under-rat, has become the superstar.

Do we love so-called "trash animals"—trash pandas, trash cats, fart squirrels—because seeing them eating blueberries at the table instead of digging through the trash makes us realize they're actually super cute? Or is it their awkwardness that makes them endearing? Are raccoons and opossums gaining a mass following because we like to root for the longshots or because we know they're bound to come out on top eventually, resilient and adaptive creatures that they are?

Maybe our love of animal outsiders has more to do with our own misfit history. It could be that we're drawn to these long-despised animals because we were on the fringes ourselves, judged by others as "lesser"—the goth kids, the nerds, the skaters, the theater geeks, the punks, or, worse, one of those who floated along the halls of high school, nearly invisible until a jock knocked you over in gym class. In any case, the early decades of the twenty-first century have taught us that traditional traits of "likeability" are poor predictors of character.

If you don't love trash animals yet, you'll find many reasons to here. Maybe it will be learning about the Japanese rats of the Edo period, or how much Beatrix Potter loved a rat she called Sammy. Maybe it will be learning more about some of the viral trash animal sensations like Louie the Raccoon, or remembering the foxes, squirrels, and badgers in Frances Hodgson Burnett's early twentieth-century classic *The Secret Garden*.

We'll start off with trading cards, where you can learn the vital stats for *Vulpes vulpes* (red fox),

Myotis lucifugus (little brown bat), and ten other trash animal favorites, learning about their habitat, their lifestyle, their diet, and what to call a group of them.

Next, we'll take a look back in history, discovering the beloved pet raccoon that roamed the White House lawn in the Roaring Twenties, as well as the starling bird that might have contributed to some of Mozart's concertos. We'll jump ahead to the furry trendsetters in the news today, including an actor in New York City who performs as Buddy the Rat, and the raccoons whose paintings help support Florida wildlife.

The Fun Facts section is a hodgepodge of trivia where we'll dig into the origin of trash animal names, take a peek into the life of bats who protect books in libraries in Portugal, find out what beavers do when they're frightened, and hear about red fox vocalizations.

In the Literature, Art, and Pop Culture section, we might be surprised to find out how many trash animals we already know through favorite shows and famous art, from the beaver in Disney's *Lady and the Tramp* to the Badger (and Rat) in *The Wind in the Willows*. We've got songs inspired by trash animals here as well, and we've squirreled away some animal expressions we can crow over, after enjoying some poetry about the squirrel from one of the foremost Transcendentalist writers of the mid-nineteenth century. We've got Resources and Inspiration for you as well. Finally, we'll find out some of the ways trash animals improve our lives and the state of the planet.

I hope this book will convince you that it's time to recast animal outcasts into a new story, recognizing that while we probably should not invite them into our home like the online influencers, we can invite them back into a shared vision of co-existence.

Perhaps what stands out the most with so many of these animals is their endless adaptability. By foraging for dinner in the trash that we create, they demonstrate their ability to make do with what is available. So often we describe them as encroaching on our space, when it's clearly the other way around. The reason so many trash animals have adapted to urban and suburban settings is because we have built these areas over the woodlands, wetlands, and grasslands that were their homes.

Some of these creatures have been here for millions of years, long before we came on the scene, and there's a good chance they may outlast us. While we're here together, let's do as much as we can to learn from these resilient creatures.

TRADING CARDS

Vital stats for trash animal fans.

VIRGINIA OPOSSUM

Didelphis virginiana

VIRGINIA OPOSSUM

Didelphis virginiana

CLASS: Mammalia

FAMILY: *Didelphidae*

FOUND: North, Central, and South America

HABITAT: Woodlands or swamps, also common in urban and suburban areas

LIFESTYLE: Nocturnal marsupials who are highly adaptable

DIET: Grass, nuts, fruits, insects, worms, birds, mice, snakes, carrion, will scavenge for pet food and through garbage

SIZE: Close to a small dog

GROUP OF: Passel

PREDATORS: Wolves, dogs, coyotes, raptors, bobcats, owls, raccoons

LIFESPAN: 1–3 years

YOUNG: Joey

TRASH ANIMAL SUPERPOWER: 

Playing dead (officially known as thanatosis)

A.K.A. **TRASH CAT**

STRIPED SKUNK

Mephitis mephitis

STRIPED SKUNK

Mephitis mephitis

CLASS: Mammalia

FAMILY: *Mephitidae*

FOUND: North America

HABITAT: Woodlands, forests, or grassy plains near forests, prefer open areas

LIFESTYLE: Nocturnal, generally solitary

DIET: Insects, fish, nuts, fruits, grass, roots, birds, small mammals, reptiles, carrion

SIZE: Close to a house cat

GROUP OF: Surfeit

PREDATORS: Red foxes, dogs, lynx, badgers, eagles, owls, crows, wolves, bobcats, and possibly coyotes

LIFESPAN: 2 years

YOUNG: Kit or skunklet

TRASH ANIMAL SUPERPOWER: ★★★☆☆

The spray, of course! When frightened, skunks emit powerful sulfur-rich compounds that shoot out of two anal glands. Plus they've got good aim!

Skunks do issue warnings before they spray—which might be a combination of hissing, raising their tail, foot stomping, charging forward, and scratching at the ground. If you miss all those signals, watch out!

A.K.A. **FART SQUIRREL**

RACCOON

Procyon lotor

RACCOON

Procyon lotor

CLASS: Mammalia

FAMILY: *Procyonidae*

FOUND: Northern part of South America through Mexico, to most of the United States and southern Canada

HABITAT: Woodlands, forests near water sources, can live in farm/rural areas, and now urban and suburban as well

LIFESTYLE: Nocturnal, promiscuous, and generally solitary

DIET: Mice, birds' eggs, fruits, insects, nuts, corn, rodents, squirrels, frogs, grasshoppers, scraps of garbage

SIZE: Close to a small dog

GROUP OF: Nursery or gaze

PREDATORS: Bobcats, coyotes, hawks, owls, red foxes

LIFESPAN: 3–5 years

YOUNG: Kit

TRASH ANIMAL SUPERPOWER: ★★★☆☆

Nimble fingers (plus they're strong swimmers and climbers and can see well in the dark)

A.K.A. **TRASH PANDA**

EASTERN GRAY SQUIRREL

Sciurus carolinensis

EASTERN GRAY SQUIRREL

Sciurus carolinensis

CLASS: Mammalia

FAMILY: Sciuridae

FOUND: Worldwide, except in Antarctica and Australia

HABITAT: Forests, urban and suburban near trees

LIFESTYLE: Diurnal or crepuscular; females nest by themselves when pregnant or caring for young

DIET: Plants, berries, seeds, nuts, insects, and will scavenge for carrion

SIZE: Larger than red squirrels and rats; 9–12 inches (23–30cm)

GROUP OF: Scurry or dray

PREDATORS: Red-tailed hawks, red foxes, weasels, gray wolves, lynx, coyotes, raccoons

LIFESPAN: 10 years

YOUNG: Kit or kitten

TRASH ANIMAL SUPERPOWER: ★☆☆☆☆

They can "speak," alerting nearby squirrels to danger

A.K.A. **TREE RAT**

NORTH AMERICAN BEAVER

Castor canadensis

NORTH AMERICAN BEAVER

Castor canadensis

CLASS: Mammalia

FAMILY: *Castoridae*

FOUND: North America

HABITAT: Freshwater (ponds, lakes, streams, rivers)

LIFESTYLE: Social with strong family structure

DIET: Herbivores who eat plants, grass, twigs, leaves

SIZE: World's second-largest rodent (after the South American capybara)

GROUP OF: Colony

PREDATORS: Wolves, coyotes, foxes, otters, great-horned owls, bobcats

LIFESPAN: up to 10 years

YOUNG: Kit (youngest), yearling (toddlers)

TRASH ANIMAL SUPERPOWER: 

Building dams (plus they can swim for 15 minutes under the water)

NORWEGIAN RAT

Rattus norvegicus

NORWEGIAN RAT

Rattus norvegicus

CLASS: Mammalia

FAMILY: *Muridae*

FOUND: Worldwide, except Antarctica

HABITAT: Forests at first, now alongside humans in a wide range of habitats, including cities and wooded areas

LIFESTYLE: Social, tend to be nocturnal

DIET: Omnivorous foragers with an enormous palate

SIZE: Bigger and heavier than mice, with a body close to 9 inches (23cm) long

GROUP OF: Mischief

PREDATORS: Skunks, weasels, cats, dogs, owls, snakes

LIFESPAN: 1–2 years

YOUNG: Pup

TRASH ANIMAL SUPERPOWER: ★★★☆☆

Eyes can go in opposite directions, and they can swim

A.K.A. **BROWN RAT, SEWER RAT, WHARF RAT, NORWAY RAT**

FERAL PIGEON

Columba livia f. domestica

FERAL PIGEON

Columba livia f. domestica

CLASS: Aves

FAMILY: *Columbidae*

FOUND: Worldwide, except Antarctica

HABITAT: Cities, farms, suburban areas, sometimes remote areas, or, in native habitats, cliffs, or mountainous areas

LIFESTYLE: Monogamous and tend to nest in communities (colonies)

DIET: Cereal grains, fruits, seeds, grasses, and whatever they can scavenge

SIZE: Bit larger than the mourning dove

GROUP OF: Flock (or in flight—a flight of pigeons)

PREDATORS: Peregrine falcon, crows, gulls, red-tailed hawk, foxes, snakes, eagles

LIFESPAN: 3–5 years

YOUNG: Squeaker or squab

TRASH ANIMAL SUPERPOWER: 

Sees in ultraviolet color and flies 50 mph (plus strong visual memory and 37 taste buds!)

A.K.A. **FLYING RAT, CITY DOVE**

EUROPEAN BADGER

Meles meles

EUROPEAN BADGER

Meles meles

CLASS: Mammalia

FAMILY: *Mustelidae*

FOUND: Throughout Europe (including U.K.)

HABITAT: Grassland, heathland, moorland, orchards, scrubland, hedges, farms, woodlands, gardens

LIFESTYLE: Nocturnal and crepuscular, very social and also quite clean, prioritizing grooming and keeping their homes (setts) neat

DIET: Primarily earthworms, as well as insects, nuts, berries, fruits, birds' eggs, and small mammals, such as hedgehogs

SIZE: Roughly the size of a Cocker Spaniel dog

GROUP OF: Cete or clan

PREDATORS: Brown bears, wolves, wolverines, lynx, eagle owls (of young badgers; adult badgers do not have known natural predators)

LIFESPAN: 5–8 years

YOUNG: Cub

TRASH ANIMAL SUPERPOWER: 

Digging burrows (elaborate underground homes called setts)

LITTLE BROWN BAT

Myotis lucifugus

LITTLE BROWN BAT

Myotis lucifugus

CLASS: Mammalia

FAMILY: *Vespertilionidae*

FOUND: Canada, United States, and some parts of Mexico

HABITAT: In winter, often shelter in caves or mines. In warmer weather they roost in trees, wood piles, buildings, and near water

LIFESTYLE: Nocturnal, hibernate in winter

DIET: Insects, including mosquitoes and moths

SIZE: 3–4 inches (7.5–10cm)

GROUP OF: Colony

PREDATORS: Cats, raccoons, snakes, hawks, weasels, owls, mice

LIFESPAN: usually 6–7 years but can live up to 30

YOUNG: Pup

TRASH ANIMAL SUPERPOWER: 

Echolocation—tracking the echoes of sounds they emit to locate their insect prey

COMMON GARTER SNAKE

Thamnophis sirtalis

COMMON GARTER SNAKE

Thamnophis sirtalis

CLASS: Reptilia

FAMILY: *Colubridae*

FOUND: North America

HABITAT: Woodlands, hillsides, marshes, meadows, prairies, near water, urban and suburban areas

LIFESTYLE: Social, adaptable, mainly diurnal, dormant in winter

DIET: Insects, earthworms, slugs, snails, crayfish, snakes, small fish, toads

SIZE: 20–30 inches (50–76cm)

GROUP OF: Den

PREDATORS: Hawks, crows, raccoons, snapping turtles, fish, other snakes

LIFESPAN: 2 years

YOUNG: Baby snakes in general are called "snakelets"

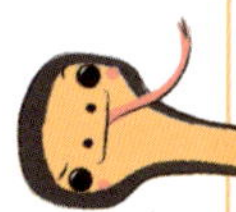

TRASH ANIMAL SUPERPOWER: 

Smell through their tongues and grow their whole lives

A.K.A. **DANGER NOODLE, NOPE ROPE**

RED FOX

Vulpes vulpes

RED FOX

Vulpes vulpes

CLASS: Mammalia

FAMILY: *Canidae*

FOUND: Throughout U.S. and Canada, the U.K., Europe, North Africa, and Asia

HABITAT: Woodland, farmland, urban areas

LIFESTYLE: Mainly nocturnal, both male and female care for the young

DIET: Fruits, rabbits, birds, field voles, worms, grain, and will scavenge for trash

SIZE: Close to a small dog

GROUP OF: Skulk or leash

PREDATORS: Bears, mountain lions, gray wolves, coyotes, eagles

LIFESPAN: Up to 3 years

YOUNG: Cubs, kits, or pups

TRASH ANIMAL SUPERPOWER: ★★★☆☆

Fantastic hearing

CARRION CROW

Corvus corone

CARRION CROW

Corvus corone

CLASS: Aves

FAMILY: *Corvidae*

FOUND: Europe and Asia

HABITAT: Coasts, marshlands, and uplands, now urban and suburban areas as well

LIFESTYLE: Monogamous for life, nest in buildings, trees, or cliffs, and forage for food

DIET: Insects, small mammals, seeds, fruit, carrion, will forage for scraps

SIZE: Smaller than a raven (20 inches/50cm length)

GROUP OF: Murder, storytelling, muster, parcel, horde

PREDATORS: Few known predators

LIFESPAN: Many live a year or less, but up to 10 in the wild

YOUNG: Infant is called corbillat

TRASH ANIMAL SUPERPOWER: ★★★★☆

Intelligence/problem-solving

HISTORY

When we think of trash animals, the image that often comes to mind is a raccoon or skunk, or red fox (depending on where you are), rummaging around in the backyard trash. Of course, our own beloved pups might be prone to this same behavior, and in fact many scholars believe "man's best friend" descended from wolves who may have been the original trash scavengers. Humans left scraps on the outer borders of early settlements, so the theories go, and wolves found an easy feast. The tamer the wolf, the closer humans allowed it to get. It may have been that gentler wolves were adopted and possibly selected to assist with tasks like hunting. Others in the field believe tamer wolves "self-selected"—cozying up to human groups and mating with other wolves who had similar less-aggressive traits. The debate as to how much the humans were domesticating the wolf and how much the wolf was "domesticating" itself is ongoing, but few seem to doubt that the act of rummaging through trash lies at the root of it.

We would never call our retrievers, beagles, or terriers trash animals now, yet the somewhat arbitrary use of the label is highlighted by their history. Fast-forward 9,000 years from the days of early civilization, and we'll find many examples of today's so-called trash animals holding places of esteem. Read on for a glimpse into some of the golden days of trash animals.

PREHISTORIC PETS

Red foxes may have been something akin to pets long before the domestication of wolves. In the early part of the twenty-first century, in the country of Jordan, archaeologists discovered the remains of a red fox buried alongside those of humans. Researchers believe evidence showing that the human and the fox had been moved together post-burial to another site indicates the fox had a special significance to the human. The burial site dates back over 16,000 years. Similar burial sites with dogs who appear to be pets have been discovered, but they appear to be only about 12,000 years old.

THE RATS OF EDO

During Japan's Edo period (1603–1868), when the country was under the rule of the Tokugawa family, "fancy" rats of different colors were bred and studied with great interest. In 1775, a guidebook on breeding fancy rats was published with the title *Yoso-tama-no-kakehashi*. A second edition was published twelve years later.

EARLY SKUNK ENCOUNTER

In 1653, when New York was called New Netherland, a Dutch naturalist wrote about a "fetid animal" he met in the woods, most likely a skunk. Fast-forward more than two centuries, and a skunk was shown in 1899 at the Bronx Zoo, the first one to make a known live appearance at an exhibition.

WOLFGANG'S STARLING

Wolfgang Amadeus Mozart had a beloved starling bird as a pet. According to the famed Austrian composer, his feathered friend could sing the beginning of his "Piano Concerto Number 17, K 453," though there is no recorded evidence for the claim. When the starling died, Mozart gave him a funeral. Some say the much-loved bird may have even influenced some of the composer's melodies.

SNAKES, SQUIRRELS, AND RACCOONS ... OH MY!

Colonists in America kept snakes, squirrels, and raccoons as pets, among other animals. Squirrels were especially popular with children. In 1773, Benjamin Franklin sympathized with his friend who lost a pet squirrel named Mungo, and even wrote an epitaph for him.

THE TALE OF BEATRIX POTTER'S RAT

Beatrix Potter had an albino rat named Samuel, A.K.A. Sammy. She dedicated her 1908 book *The Tale of Samuel Whiskers* to the pet, with the following inscription: *"In Remembrance of 'Sammy,' The intelligent Pink-Eyed Representative of a persecuted (but irrepressible) race. An affectionate little friend, and most accomplished thief!"* (The book was originally called *The Roly-Poly Pudding.*) Potter's drawing of Sammy can be found in the Victoria and Albert Museum in London, England, with the amusing title: "The peculiar dream of Mr. Samuel Whiskers upon the subject of Dutch cheese."

SQUIRREL REFERRAL

In her 1851 book *Domestic Pets: Their Habits and Management*, Jane Loudon gives a glimpse of the domestic life of squirrels in nineteenth-century America:

> *"The squirrel is a beautiful little creature, very agile and graceful in its movements, and extremely docile. Though not so intelligent as the dog, it may be taught to jump from one hand to the other to search for a hidden nut, &c.; and it soon knows its name, and the persons who feed it. It is, indeed, capable of affection, though not to the same degree as the dog or the cat … If, however, a squirrel has never been in a perfectly wild state, it may easily be made quite tame and domestic, and may be suffered to roam about the room without there being any danger of its wishing to make its escape."*

We can learn more about how the squirrel fit into the nineteenth-century household from the 1883 household guide *Every Day*

Home Advice Relating Chiefly to Household Management with Hints Upon Houses, how to Construct and Preserve; Domestic Cookery in All Its Departments ... Together with Hints Upon Nearly Every Emergency that Arises During the Lifetime of Man, Woman Or Child. Squirrels are given their own section in the chapter on "Domestic Pets," with a short entry:

> *"Not difficult to tame and very amusing as domestic pets. Squirrels require but slight care beyond the keeping of their cages thoroughly clean and sweet, and regularly supplying them with food, which consists of nuts, fruit, seeds, and bread crumbs. They seldom breed in captivity. They may be bought at the bird-fanciers'."*

SHE WADDLES IN BEAUTY

The British Romantic poet Lord Byron at one time had a badger, a peacock, and a host of other "pets." His most famous "weird pet" story is the bear he kept while he was a student at Trinity College, Dublin, in Ireland. The campus prohibited dogs, so the pet bear was his workaround!

RACCOON IN THE HOUSE

The 30th President of the United States, Calvin Coolidge, was called "Silent Cal," but one imagines his White House must have been anything but, given the number of pets he had. Perhaps the raccoon named Rebecca was the most famous, and she was accompanied by bears, a bobcat, a wallaby, and a pygmy hippo, among other animals. Rebecca the Raccoon was sent as a gift to be consumed for Thanksgiving dinner in 1926, but the family had other ideas, deciding to let her stay on as a guest. Coolidge's wife Grace was particularly fond of Rebecca, sometimes bringing her around town with a collar that let everyone know she wasn't just any raccoon but the "White House Raccoon." When the family left D.C., they gave Rebecca to what is now the National Zoo.

NEW WORLD MONSTER

Students of history may know the year 1492 as the date when Columbus sailed across the ocean to the "New World" (searching for India), but it was also the year when one of his commanders came upon an opossum in Brazil, which he compared to a fox but called a "Monster." He described the unusual creature: "the hinder a Monkey, the feet were like a Mans, with Ears like an Owl; under whose Belly hung a great Bag, in which it carry'd the Young," then proceeded to take it back alive to King Ferdinand of Spain. Explorer and naturalist John Lawson called the animal "the Wonder of all the Land-Animals" when he observed one in North America around 1700.

VICTORIAN RATCATCHER

The story of the Pied Piper has its origins in medieval Germany, but rats were still a major problem hundreds of years later, even in Victorian London. Rats had arrived in London the century before and had become a significant public health issue by the time of Queen Victoria. In fact, one man claimed the title of the Queen's personal ratcatcher. Jack Black from Battersea, England, had no fear of rats and began catching them in childhood, making a show of his captures that attracted passers-by. His talent was for catching *live rats*, not just getting rid of them. Some he bred for spectacles called rat-baiting, where dogs were matched against rats, and others he turned into pet "fancy rats."

While rats have long been blamed for bringing the centuries-long plague (A.K.A. Black Death) to Europe, new research indicates that it was in fact people who were responsible for spreading the disease that killed approximately 25 million. Studies conducted at the University of Oslo showed that outbreaks were likely due to lice and fleas that lived on humans. Perhaps we owe rats a belated apology?

TRASH ANIMALS
IN THE NEWS

Welcome to the era of the eccentric animal outsider! Meet the lovable cast-offs who have captured the attention of thousands in the news and in social media. Raccoons eating dinner, rats cuddled together for an afternoon nap, an opossum mom exploring the backyard with her kids—the world is awash with photos and stories about these adorable once-rejected pets living their best lives. In this chapter we'll meet the rescues, the rehabilitated, and the nocturnal freeloaders who became the leaders of the pack.

LOUIE THE RACCOON

Louie the Raccoon lived in South Florida and had over half a million followers on Instagram. A beloved animal and friend, Louie passed away in April of 2025, having touched the hearts of many. His mom, Jaime Arslan, didn't plan to turn her *Procyon* sidekick into an online *verminfluencer*. She met the masked sensation when she was volunteering for a wildlife rescue as a way to help her cope with the recent loss of her father. Louie couldn't survive in the wild, so in 2021 he came to Arslan's home in Miami-Dade.

Arslan, who cared for three other raccoons as well (Lea, Leo, and Lucy), hopes the Instagram page can help reshape the public's impression of raccoons. After all, what trash animal wears a red beret and sits at the table?

With tags like #raccoonsofinstagram, #trash-panda, #raccoon love, and #raccoonlife, the Insta page showed Louie in holiday hats, eating snacks, stealing snacks, lounging in bed, sprawled out, curled up, climbing a tree, playing with toys, and swimming. The "fashionista," as his mom called

PIZZA RAT:

In 2015, a video of a real rat carrying a slice of pizza down the subway stairs went viral, becoming known as "pizza rat" and viewed millions of times. Comic Matt Little had filmed the video on his cell phone, and overnight #pizzarat went viral. The incident

him, even liked to play on a playground. In 2024 Louie the Raccoon won the title of 2024 Cadbury Bunny award. (Previous winners include Crash the Rescue Cat [2023] and Betty the Frog [2021].)

Oh, and Louie the Raccoon painted! Proceeds from the sale of his paintings went to a Florida-based wildlife sanctuary.

Arslan, formerly a veterinary technician, had the proper permit and expertise for her animals. She reminds the public, however, that raccoons are wild animals.

captured the imagination of newscasters and late-show hosts, including Stephen Colbert on *The Late Show*, who brought up the story of "urban wildlife," joking about made-up creatures Pasta Opossum and Calzone Pigeon.

BTW, Pizza Rat has been made into various holiday ornaments, including one titled NYC's "unofficial mascot," available at the Museum of the City of New York. (Just in case you're wondering where the rat's loyalty lies, he's wearing the iconic I love NY t-shirt.)

BUDDY THE RAT

Jonathan Lyons is an actor (and once puppeteer) who moonlights around New York City performing as Buddy the Rat. Videos of Buddy playing the piano, scrambling around Washington Square Park's fountain, and dancing with others in front of a giant pigeon sculpture at 30th Street and 10th Avenue near Hudson Yards (see "Giant Pigeon" on page 57) have attracted more than 1.4 million subscribers on YouTube and 157,000 followers on Instagram. Partially inspired by rats recast as endearing creatures on Instagram, and by the real-life Pizza Rat (see page 52), Lyons was inspired during the Covid pandemic to try a street performance idea. He made his mask by hand—"a hand-sculpted clay design," as he calls it—trying out a prototype with cardboard first.

Artist Nicola Russell, who posts on Instagram at vangoghandloveyourself, admires Lyons' work, which she sees as more than a "gimmick," communicating "... how we dismiss rats as dirty or evil when they are so similar to humans. Intelligent, social, and ruthlessly survivors." Her "Portrait of Buddy the Rat" is an oil on canvas featuring Lyons in his famous costume, sitting human-like in a chair in the artist's studio.

PUMPKIN THE RACCOON

Pumpkin the Raccoon was a beloved rescue raised near the beautiful turquoise waters of the Atlantic on the Bahamas coast. As a baby, Pumpkin fell out of a tree in the yard of Rosie Kemp and was abandoned by her mother. There was no shelter that could take her in, so Kemp and her daughter Laura Young brought "Pumps" into their lives. Young nursed to health the baby raccoon with a broken leg and catapulted her to online fame. Eventually Young, her husband, and their two rescue dogs became Pumpkin's family, and Pumpkin fit right in.

Although the celebrity raccoon passed away in 2019, the "lover of mischief," as CNN called her, lived a happy life, documented both online and in the 2016 book, *Pumpkin: The Raccoon Who Thought*

She Was a Dog, published by St. Martin's Griffin and written by her owner. Money raised by the photos of Pumpkin eating pancakes or pizza, cuddling with the dogs, and involved in all kinds of other fun antics, helped donate funds to World Central Kitchen, along with other charities.

"Pumps"—the Queen Bee of trash animal internet fame—died at almost five years old, a huge loss to her fans and to her mom, most of all, who wrote the following tribute on Pumpkin's Instagram page: *"She ignited my creative side, which I had suppressed for so long and dared me to believe that maybe, just maybe, I could start believing in myself and give my dreams a chance."*

Raccoons sometimes make an appearance on Manhattan Bird Alert on X (formerly known as Twitter).

GIANT PIGEON

You might expect to find many pigeons on a trip to New York City, but perhaps not the 16-foot-high aluminum sculpture called "Dinosaur" on display on the New York City's High Line. The thought-provoking piece of art seems to ask: Who gets to keep watch over the city from on high?

Like all birds today, pigeons are descendants of dinosaurs that roamed for 165 million years during the Mesozoic Era, going extinct approximately 66 million years ago. The sculpture created by artist Iván Argote,

PIGEON FEST:

Pigeon Fest, a full-day festival celebrating National Pigeon Appreciation Day and centering around Dinosaur himself, held its inaugural event in June 2025. In addition to events including carnival games, workshops, and a concert, this included the first High Line's Pigeon Impersonation Pageant. Contestants were judged on plumage costume, strut, and sound by a panel of experts.

who grew up in Bogotá, Colombia (and currently lives in Paris), pays tribute in an unexpected way to the immigrant bird who may have come to the city for the first time in the nineteenth century, like many immigrants to the city. Domesticated at the time of their arrival, pigeons were prized for their ability to carry messages that relied on their homing instinct. In both World Wars, pigeons contributed immensely by serving as messengers in battle (see Fun Facts, page 84).

Argote provided a glimpse into the thought process behind the unusual statue. "Like them, one day we won't be around anymore, but perhaps a remnant of humanity will live on—as pigeons do—in the dark corners and gaps of future worlds. I feel this sculpture could generate an uncanny feeling of attraction, seduction, and fear among the inhabitants of New York."

The sculpture will be on display from October 2024 to the spring of 2026.

FAN CLUBS

Facebook has a public group with over 20,000 members called Squirrel Lovers. Group moderators describe it as "... the ultimate community for anyone who adores these fascinating creatures. Whether you're a seasoned squirrel enthusiast or new to the charm of these furry friends, our group is the perfect place to share, learn, and connect." The page is a place

Santonio-based artist Amanda Lanford has a section on her website called Trash Animals where she clarifies that eating garbage doesn't mean that's what you are. Squirrels, prairie dogs, porcupines, bats, raccoons, and opossums are among the animals she features in her artwork. Lanford says she has a special interest in bringing attention to "creatures that often go unnoticed, or worse—get dismissed as pests."

to share "Sightings and Stories," "Tips & Tricks," "Educational Insights," "Squirrel Arts & Crafts," "Support & Conservation," "Global Community," and more.

There are raccoon, fox, pigeon, and rat fan clubs on Facebook as well, including one dedicated to the red fox specifically called "Red Fox Lover," as well as the Companion Pigeon Club with over 49,000 members. "The Rat Fan Club," with over 75,000 members, was originally a newsletter sent monthly by Debbie Ducommun called "The Rat Report." Debbie (A.K.A. "The Rat Lady") wrote several books about rats in addition to her newsletter.

Established in January of 1976, the National Fancy Rat Society pre-dates all the Facebook fan pages, although it maintains a page on Facebook now featuring updates on its shows.

STARFISH THE OPOSSUM

Opossums have a lot going for them: They are the only native marsupials in the United States. They have survived for millions of years, virtually unchanged. Their low body temperature makes them almost completely resistant to rabies. And like their cousins the possums, they can play dead to avoid capture or threat. Oft-confused, the opossum and possum are both tree-bound marsupials;

In the fall of 2022, BBC Wildlife offered suggestions for the best gifts for badger lovers, including an "I love Badgers" tote bag from the Mammal Society and a "Festive Forest Mug" featuring a badger alongside other woodland creatures designed by Sophie Allport.

however, the opossum has a gray-white body and white face and hairless tail and is limited to the Americas. The possum is more likely found "Down Under" and can be spotted in a variety of colors.

Until recently the opossum's bad rep as a menace has kept it out of the spotlight and deep underground. But thanks to the love of the underdog and ubiquitous presence of social media, that has changed. Opossums are the new llama, or unicorn, or sloth—and with a growing social media in the millions, that place is here to stay.

"Has anyone met Starfish, the Instagram-famous opossum from NOLA?" one such thread implores.

Starfish has nearly a quarter of a million followers on Instagram and Facebook combined. When her human arranges meet-and-greets (annual pilgrimages for Starfish's admirers), they come to pay homage to their celebrity in droves, sporting opossum attire and themed swag, such as charm bracelets, prayer candles, headwear, jewelry, and tattoos.

PEANUT

We've all seen squirrels collecting acorns, but Peanut the Squirrel collected quite a following on Instagram, at peanut_the_squirrel12, an account with almost a million followers, with numbers increasing dramatically after his death. Peanut lived on a farm with his friend Fred

Time Out New York did a feature in May of 2023 on the city's wildlife that included raccoons and pigeons (along with the humpback whale and bottlenose dolphin).

the Raccoon in Pine City, New York, not far from the Pennsylvania border, and loved to jump into his owners' hands, grab onto their clothes, and eat waffles with them.

Sadly, both Peanut and Fred were seized by the state's Environmental Conservation team after complaints that the owners did not have proper licenses and may have been keeping the wildlife in unsafe conditions. Peanut was euthanized as part of a rabies test, leaving a hole in the heart of squirrel-lovers everywhere. As adorable and gentle as Peanut proved to be, squirrels cannot be kept as pets in New York State. Rehabilitators can care for squirrels on a temporary basis with the proper license, but they must return the animals to the wilderness—a tough lesson for those that loved him.

BACK TO THE WILD

A wildlife rehabilitation center in New York encourages followers of its Instagram account not to keep wildlife as pets themselves. Owner Nancy Coyne shows fans the animals she cares for on the page and the progress that they make toward the day when they can be released back into the wild. A beaver examining pots and pans in the kitchen or riding a kayak, a baby raccoon being held in her hand, a lethargic skunk found in somebody's yard, and a beaver practicing dam-making—all an ordinary day-in-the-life for Coyne. Fans can follow the adventures on Raising the Wild on YouTube.

Coyne started rescuing domestic animals and moved on to fostering farm animals. Her rescue "Beave"—"The Internet's Most Famous Beaver"—became a sensation on TikTok when she started using stuffed animals and whatever else she could find to build "dams." Coyne's daughter had taught her about TikTok, suggesting she feature the beaver on there, and created the account.

Coyne went on *Weekend Edition* for an interview with Lulu Garcia-Navarro to share their story, where she talks about being able to recognize the moment when she knows it's time to let the animals go. "He will become aggressive. He will distance himself from me and then I will know that it's time for him to move on." Sounds a bit like raising a teenager!

READY, SET, SELFIE

French photographer Augustin Lignier was intrigued by the addictive nature of sharing pictures of our lives online, and in particular the selfie habit. Receiving a cue from American psychologist B. F. Skinner (whose lever experiment is one of the most famous in psychology), Lignier gave two rats from

the pet shop the chance to take pictures of themselves by pressing a button. As a reward to Augustin (named for himself) and Arthur (named for his brother), Lignier offered sugar. The reward ultimately became intermittent (the most compelling kind), and the rats eventually lost interest in the sugar and seemed to become addicted to the behavior of pressing the button. (Although Lignier initially showed the rats the adorable pictures they were taking, he doesn't think they responded to the photos.) Lignier likens the rats' behavior to humans becoming addicted first to the dopamine hits of social media and eventually to the behavior itself.

A NOTE ON TRASH ANIMAL PETS:

Besides the fact that it may not be legal to own a raccoon, squirrel, opossum, or other wild animal as a pet depending on where you live, wild animals as pets carry health concerns and potential risks to people or other pets. Any injured animal should always be handled by a wildlife rehabilitator. It is never legal to capture a wild animal and bring it home as a pet.

FUN FACTS

Humans growing crops have used a version of modern-day scarecrows from as far back as ancient Greece, when farmers in approximately 2500 BCE carved a figure of a god to protect their vineyards by frightening birds away.

• • •

Chiroptera, the scientific name for bats, means "hand wing" from the Greek "*chiro*" (hand) and "*ptera*" (wing).

• • •

In France, young pigeon (squab), a favorite in Medieval times, is still a popular dish.

Bats are one of the oldest species of mammals on Earth. Fossils show they have been around for over 50 million years, a recent addition compared to the horseshoe crab, who came on the scene roughly 445 million years ago. On the other end, humans are just joining the party—we have been in existence for somewhere between 250,000 and 300,000 years.

• • •

Boxing champion Mike Tyson is a big fan of pigeons and even credits his love of the humble bird with potentially kick-starting his professional boxing career. In an article he wrote for *The New York Times* in 2011, he shared the origin of his fondness for the ubiquitous city bird: "As a child, I was very awkward and never felt as though I fit in (anywhere). On the roof, none of my insecurities mattered. As I watched the birds soar above me, in that moment I was free just like them." When a neighborhood bully killed a pigeon, Tyson responded with swift justice, a fight that made him think losing the pigeon "... was the catalyst to the fighter within."

The University of Wisconsin thinks highly of the lowly badger—their mascot is Bucky Badger (full name: Buckingham Ulysses Badger).

• • •

Beaver kits and yearlings play together, and older siblings have been known to help out by taking care of younger ones.

• • •

Giant beavers roamed the Earth during the Ice Age.

Garter snakes have friends! Research published in the April 2020 volume of *Behavioral Ecology and Sociobiology* provided evidence "that these snakes actively seek out social interaction and prefer to join and remain with larger groups and that their social interaction patterns are influenced by consistent individual differences in boldness and sociability."

• • •

Opossums are immune to some snakebite venom. Scientists are studying the protein that resists snake venom with the hope of contributing to snake bite intervention. (Snake bites are a major global health issue.)

• • •

Australia is home to possums (without the o). Both marsupials, they are very different animals.

There are more than 1,300 different species of bats in the world! (In fact, 20 percent of the world's mammals are bats.)

• • •

Beavers will slap their tails on the water when they are frightened, to send a warning out to other beavers of possible danger.

• • •

Snakes as pets goes back to at least the ancient world. In ancient Greece they symbolized health, protection, and transition.

Baby raccoons make a sound called "chattering" to let their moms know they want a drink.

• • •

Female opossums (Jills) raise the young (Joeys) without the help of the males (Jacks). When the Joeys outgrow the pouch, their moms carry them around on their backs until they're ready to be on their own, when they're about four months old.

The name raccoon may have come from the Algonquin word "*ahrah-koon-em*," which describes the rubbing or scratching motion of the animal's hands, or the Powatan "*aroughcun*," which describes "one scratching with his hands." The scientific name *Procyon lotor* translates approximately to dog-like washer. (In Swedish biologist Carl Linnaeus' taxonomy, the handsy animal was originally compared to a bear.) The Italian *orsetto lavatore* and French *raton laveur* both refer to the animal's cleaning ritual as well. Although raccoons appear to clean their food, scientists have determined that they are not washing so much as exploring the food to learn about it.

Pigeons held a special place in the heart of Serbian-American engineer, physicist, and inventor Nikola Tesla. When he wasn't discovering the rotating magnetic field, he was caring for domesticated pigeons in his hotel room. Of one particular favorite he wrote, "That pigeon was the joy of my life. If she needed me, nothing else mattered. As long as I had her, there was a purpose in my life."

• • •

A garter snake once gave birth to 98 babies! Usually, these non-venomous creatures give birth to between 15 and 40 babies at a time, one of the few snake species who give birth live. And mama snakes waste no time postpartum. The snakelets are on their own when it comes to hunting for food as soon as they are born.

Stink badgers are also known as false badgers and are classified as skunks (part of the *Mephitidae* family). They are found in Malaysia, Indonesia, and the Philippines.

• • •

Newborn opossums (Joeys) are tiny—comparable in size to a honeybee, or even a grain of rice!

• • •

Raccoons are the largest mammals in the *Procyonidae* family. Other species in this tree-climbing family aren't quite as well-known and include the coati, olingo, New World ringtail, and the kinkajou, among others.

• • •

Viviparous refers to a species that gives birth live, as opposed to oviparous, which gives birth to eggs first, as most snakes do.

The origin of the name for Chicago might be a French version of the Miami-Illinois Native American word "*shikaakwa*," which has two meanings: striped skunk and smelly onion. The plant called Stink Onion grew along the Chicago River.

• • •

The red fox has more than 20 different vocalizations, including calls described as barks, screams, and a noise that sounds like whining. Little foxes (kits) have their own distinct sounds as well. Fox sounds can be heard at: https://wildambience.com/wildlife-sounds/red-fox.

• • •

A Siberian bat lived to at least 41 years old, the longest lifespan recorded for the only flying mammal. (Flying squirrels can soar quite nicely, but their flight path is thought of more as gliding than actual flight.)

Opossums are highly resistant to rabies, a stroke of luck that is believed to be related to their low temperature.

• • •

American badgers have been known to share hunting duties with coyotes.

• • •

Archaeologists have found 5,000-year-old images of pigeons in Mesopotamia (modern-day Iran).

Ernest Thompson Seton, a twentieth-century naturalist, offered a poetic description of the skunk's smell in Life-histories of Northern Animals, published in 1910: *"Those who have never smelled it may realize some of its power if they imagine a mixture of perfume musk, essence of garlic, burning sulphur and sewer gas, intensified a thousand times. It is so strong that under certain circumstances it can be smelled for miles down wind."*

• • •

In the same book mentioned above—*Life-histories of Northern Animals*—Ernest Thompson Seton offers a chapter on the Royal fox, Prairie Red-fox or Common Red-fox of Manitoba (*Vulpes regalis*, a subspecies of the red fox). Seton tells an amusing story of a fox who had left a garter-snake "bitten ... nearly in two" out on the snow. Based on what he observed, Seton imagined that the fox left the snake in case he could not find anything better, but happily came upon two prairie-chickens further on his jaunt. With the chickens he had a good-enough meal that *"he was not compelled to go back for the cold snake, which is never good eating, and on a cold day would have been a very cold lunch indeed."*

The name squirrel comes from the Greek Σκίουρος, which translates to "*skiouros*," from "*skia*" for shadow and "*oura*" for tail. The Latin *Sciuridae* is the family name for squirrel that we continue to use today.

• • •

Early French settlers in Canada called skunks "*l'enfant du diable*"—child of the devil.

• • •

Snakes' bodies are the same temperature as their immediate environment, making them ectotherms.

Usually, we think about protecting ourselves from bats, but in Portugal, some bats are the ones doing the protecting. Two libraries built in the eighteenth century—Biblioteca Joanina and the Mafra Palace Library—depend on tiny bats to eat any insects that might otherwise harm the libraries' precious collections. Apparently, the bats may have been keeping the bugs at bay for centuries. If you are lucky enough to spend an evening at Biblioteca Joanina, you might have the good fortune to catch sight of one of the winged guards, members of the colony of common pipistrelle.

• • •

Of all the world's foxes, the red fox is the biggest. (The tiny fennec fox of North Africa is the smallest. However, their ears are enormous, giving them a batlike appearance!)

Pigeons came from birds domesticated 6,000 years ago and are related to the doves of the Bible's Old and New Testaments.

HOW CAN YOU TELL A CROW FROM A RAVEN?

They're both jet-black birds in the *Corvidae* family, but ravens are larger, with a tail that has a wedge shape compared to the square shape of a crow's tail. Ravens also have a deeper, throatier call.

Each bird breed has its own call. Crows make a "caw," and ravens make a croaking sound.

In the final battles of World War I, a pigeon named Cher Ami saved the lives of 194 soldiers by successfully delivering a desperate message for help, even after being shot.

• • •

Opossums have 50 teeth. (The giant armadillo—*Priodontes maximus*—can have up to 100 teeth, the most for any mammal. Great white sharks might get up to 300 choppers at any one time. But the snail has the most of all—around 14,000.)

• • •

Before teenagers had to deal with insults about braces on their teeth, beavers were the original metal mouths. Most of us know beavers have powerful teeth (and, as with squirrels' teeth, they never stop growing!), but it might be a surprise to learn they are orange. The iron in their enamel coating gives beavers' teeth their orange hue.

The word rodent is derived from the Latin word "*rodere*", meaning "to gnaw."

• • •

Although John James Audubon was a French-American wildlife artist and naturalist, he was interested in the opossum at least partly in terms of its food value, calling it an "excellent substitute for roast pig."

• • •

The most common snake in North America is—you guessed it—the garter snake!

• • •

Most people born after elastic socks became popular aren't too familiar with garters, but they were once used to hold up men's slippery socks. They also lent their name to the familiar garter snake, also called "garden snake" by mistake.

Badgers are in the *Mustelidae* family, which also includes minks, weasels, otters, and wolverines.

• • •

The rats used in medical labs are descendants of Norwegian rats, selected for their plenitude, ease of breeding, and their ability to flourish in captivity.

• • •

Crows have a strategy of gathering together to fend off enemies, and the behavior has an official name: *mobbing*. The technique may include loud caws alongside various physical acts of intimidation. Other birds, including blue jays, also engage in mobbing against threats.

• • •

Norwegian rats' teeth are so strong, they can chew through cinder block.

Polar ice, tundra, and deserts are the only places on Earth you won't find rats.

• • •

Rare, pink-eyed albino squirrels have made their home in Olney, Illinois, for over a century. Each year the city holds an annual White Squirrel Count in the fall. In 2024 the count was 81 (compared to just over 1,000 gray). An instructor at a community college in town feared the rare squirrel would become extinct and kicked off the annual count as part of his research to preserve the squirrel in 1977. Only a few towns in the U.S. have white squirrel populations—some, albino squirrels, like in Olney, and others leucistic white squirrels. In the former, melanin production is blocked, whereas in the leucistic variety a mutation gives rise to the white fur, but the eyes are not red or pink as they are in albino squirrels.

The rat is the first animal of the Chinese Zodiac calendar. According to Chinese legend, the rat won the race called by the Emperor (or possibly Buddha) to determine which animals would become part of the Zodiac.

Scientists wondered if crows would have different behavioral test results depending on whether they knew the test administrator. Would a human-animal relationship impact the experiment? The title of a study published in 2013 reveals that indeed it did: *Familiarity with the experimenter influences the performance of Common ravens* (Corvus corax) *and Carrion crows* (Corvus corone) *in cognitive tasks.*

Rats can move their whiskers one at a time. By "whisking," they can explore their environment and take in sensory information.

In 2018 an organization called the Squirrel Census led a count of Eastern gray squirrels in New York City's Central Park. Over 300 people contributed to the citizen science project, which determined that the park had approximately 2,300 Eastern gray squirrels, a species introduced to the park in the 1870s. (The shop at the Squirrel Census website sells maps visualizing the results of the study, along with an "Official Central Park Squirrel Census" T-shirt, and other related gifts.)

• • •

European badgers are larger and more social than American badgers. In areas with dense badger populations, you'll often find these animals in Europe sharing their resources. In Italy, badgers may even extend the den invitation to other species, such as red foxes and porcupines!

"I smell a rat" means something is wrong, but giant "HeroRATS" use their keen sense of smell to fight the good fight. An inventive nonprofit called APOPO trains giant rats to combat deadly diseases and track down hidden explosives. An African giant pouched rat named Carolina identified over 3,000 cases of tuberculosis in Ethiopia and Tanzania during her seven-year career. (As of November 2024, she has been enjoying retirement.) In just one year, it is estimated that the HeroRATS prevented around 400,000 cases of tuberculosis. Meanwhile, Ronin, another "HeroRAT" of the same breed as Carolina, holds a Guinness World Record for his work sniffing out landmines and explosives in Cambodia.

LITERATURE, ART, AND POP CULTURE

They inspired artists like Picasso, beguiled Native Americans, and lend their wily selves to many an English idiom. Plus, you'll be surprised at how many trash animals show up as beloved literary figures, and children's movies are full of iconic versions of bats, badgers, and more.

“Everything is made out of Magic, leaves and trees, flowers and birds, badgers and foxes and squirrels and people. So it must be all around us. In this garden—in all the places.”
—*The Secret Garden, Frances Hodgson Burnett* (1911)

The Northern Cherokee Nation have a story about an opossum who lost his tail:

At first it was long and full, and he was overly proud and boastful of it. Rabbit grew envious and planned a trick on Opossum, getting Cricket to clip away at the tail, pretending he was helping Opossum to get ready for a dance. Cricket wrapped the clipped hair in a ribbon so Opossum wouldn't notice it was gone until the big reveal at the dance in front of all the animals. Opossum was so upset and embarrassed when he showed his missing tail that he played dead.

THE ADVENTURES OF RICK RACCOON

The first raccoon that many kids in the U.S. encounter is the lovable character Ranger Rick, who first appeared when the National Wildlife Federation published *The Adventures of Rick Raccoon* in 1959. Creator J. A. "Ash" Brownridge hoped stories about animals banding together to clean fresh water sources would help children understand the importance of the organization's mission. A monthly magazine called *Ranger Rick's Nature Magazine* followed, starting in 1967. Somewhere along the way the name shortened to *Ranger Rick*®, but the magazine is still going strong.

PICASSO'S PIGEONS

In the mid-twentieth century, famed Spanish painter Pablo Picasso painted a series of nine oil paintings celebrating the wild pigeons he could see from his workshop in the South of France. The paintings were part of a larger series called *Las Meninas,* which was a comprehensive study and re-interpretation of a work by Spanish painter Diego Velázquez with the same name. *Las Meninas* —The Maids of Honor—was an oil painting Velázquez created in 1656 during the Spanish Baroque period. The windows in Picasso's paintings may also have been a nod to French artist Henri Matisse, who had once given Picasso white Milanese pigeons as a gift. (BTW, researchers found evidence that pigeons can distinguish between art by Monet and Picasso.)

PET SQUIRREL

In Gallery 755 at The Metropolitan Museum of Art in New York City, visitors can view a painting by John Singleton Copley called *Daniel Crommelin Verplanck*. The 1771 painting shows the boy in the painting's title at age nine with his pet squirrel, who is wearing a gold chain.

"THE MOUNTAIN AND THE SQUIRREL" by Ralph Waldo Emerson (1846)

The mountain and the squirrel
Had a quarrel,
And the former called the latter
"Little prig."
Bun replied,
"You are doubtless very big;
But all sorts of things and weather
Must be taken in together
To make up a year
And a sphere.
And I think it no disgrace
To occupy my place.
If I'm not so large as you,
You are not so small as I,
And not half so spry:
I'll not deny you make
A very pretty squirrel track.
Talents differ; all is well and wisely put;
If I cannot carry forests on my back,
Neither can you crack a nut."

FROM TRASH TO TREASURE

Raccoons have been creating their own artwork in recent years. Human owners of raccoons Piper and Cheeto noticed how much their pets used their hands to touch things and take in information throughout the day. The owners thought painting would be a great channel for those busy hands. Piper and Cheeto's paintings now sell for between $150 and $200 at titotheraccoon.com/shop.

Top 10 Outcast Animal Characters

1. Batman—DC Comic Superhero (Bruce Wayne by day) who first arrived in 1939 in DETECTIVE COMICS #27. (If you want to be an avenger in disguise, what costume would you pick? The one that scares you most! Fans say that's what Bruce Wayne did in choosing a bat for his alter-ego. Wayne had a lifelong fear of the creature stemming from a childhood confrontation that made him think a batman would make a formidable assailant.)

2. Pepé Le Pew—a Warner Bros. character cartoon skunk by Chuck Jones for Looney Tunes and Merrie Melodies cartoons. The comic creation came on the scene in 1945 and was known for his terribly boundary-violating chase of Penelope Pussycat and other love interests. (Today Pepé Le Pew has become a controversial character for his behavior and lack of consent.)

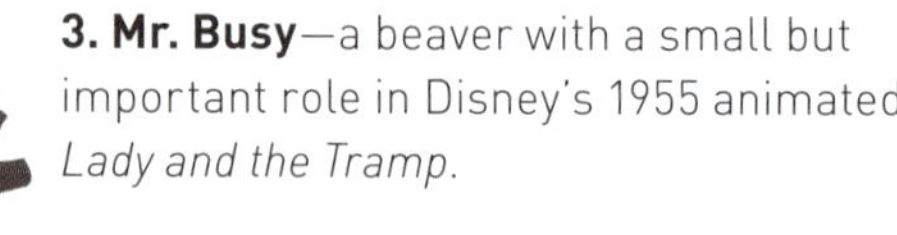

3. Mr. Busy—a beaver with a small but important role in Disney's 1955 animated *Lady and the Tramp*.

4. Master Viper—a green tree viper in the animated movie *Kung Fu Panda*, produced by DreamWorks, part of the Furious Five group.

5. Friar Tuck—a badger, one of the Merry Men in Disney's 1973 animated classic movie *Robin Hood*. (In this version, Robin Hood and Maid Marian are both foxes.)

6. Mr. Fox—a red fox in the 2009 animated film *Fantastic Mr. Fox* by Wes Anderson, based on the Roald Dahl novel published in 1970.

7. Pogo the Possum—a comic strip star created by Walt Kelly in 1948, Pogo was once syndicated in 450 newspapers for more than 25 years. (Pogo's famous line—"We have met the enemy and he is us"—was a takeoff of a famous quote from Commodore Oliver Hazard Perry after the Battle of Lake Erie: "We have met the enemy and they are ours." The words were spoken on September 10, 1813, during the War of 1812. Before the phrase was used in the series cartoon, Walt Kelly created a poster for the first Earth Day in 1970, showing Pogo surveying trash in an orchard.

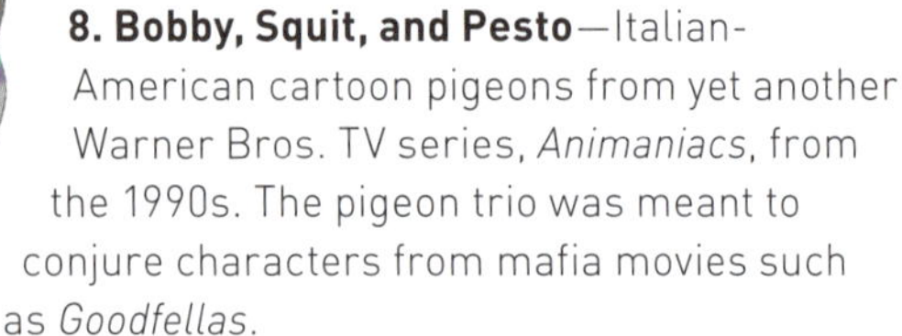

8. Bobby, Squit, and Pesto—Italian-American cartoon pigeons from yet another Warner Bros. TV series, *Animaniacs*, from the 1990s. The pigeon trio was meant to conjure characters from mafia movies such as *Goodfellas*.

9. Norvirus Raccoon—the main character from the 2014 animated film, *The Nut Job*. Norvirus was played by iconic actor Liam Neeson.

10. Jake—the only real animal on the list. Jake was the pet crow of Brooks Hatlen (James Whitmore), featured in the 1994 prison drama, *The Shawshank Redemption*.

BACCALAUREATE

Twentieth-century American poet and lawyer Archibald MacLeish brings pigeons into his celebrated poem "Baccalaureate."

The fog that creeps in wanly from the sea,
The rotton harbor smell, the mystery
Of moonlit elms, the flash of pigeon wings,
The sunny Green, the old-world peace that clings
About the college yard, where endlessly
The dead go up and down. These things shall be
Enchantment of our heart's rememberings.
—From *Baccalaureate* by Archibald MacLeish.

BEATRIX POTTER WAS A MASSIVE TRASH ANIMAL FAN

As a child, Potter had many unusual pets, including a snake named Sally.

In addition to the story inspired by the rat she cherished as an adult (see History, p. 43), Beatrix Potter gave squirrels their due when she published *The Tale of Squirrel Nutkin* in 1903.

> *"This is a Tale about a tail—a tail that belonged to a little red squirrel, and his name was Nutkin.*
>
> *He had a brother called Twinkleberry, and a great many cousins: they lived in a wood at the edge of a lake."*

In 1912, Potter gave a nod to two more trash animals with *The Tale of Mr. Tod*, where Peter Rabbit and Benjamin Bunny must contend with a badger named Tommy Brock and a fox named Mr. Tod.

> *"I have made many books about well-behaved people. Now, for a change, I am going to make a story about two disagreeable people, called Tommy Brock and Mr. Tod."*

Outcast Animal Expressions

Badger—To pester, hound, or repeatedly nag.

Badger game—A type of extortion where a woman lures a man into an awkward or compromising situation, where he is blackmailed by someone pretending to be her husband.

Badger the witness—Insult and antagonize the witness on the other side.

Busy as a beaver—Super busy.

Crow over—To brag about, especially about defeating someone else.

Eager beaver—Someone ready to work hard (sometimes a bit irritating in the eagerness).

Eat crow—Like eating one's words, but with a greater sense of shame; humbly admitting one was in the wrong.

Fox—A shrewd, strategic, crafty person or an attractive person (also crafty as a fox, sly as a fox, cunning as a fox, wily as a fox—apparently foxes are seen as quite capable animals!).

Fox in the henhouse—A sneaky person planning to take advantage of their situation to prey on others.

I smell a rat—To sense that something isn't right, perhaps someone is being deceived.

Let everyone skin his own skunk—Everyone should take care of their own responsibilities (especially perhaps an unpleasant task).

Rat—Someone who can't be trusted.

Rat out—Blow the whistle on bad behavior, to tell on someone.

Rats!—An expression of annoyance (like, damn!).

Skunk—A name for beer that has been overexposed to light. (There has been a long-standing myth that beer once chilled and then removed from the fridge will "skunk," but the myth has fortunately been debunked.)

Snake in the grass—A false friend or traitorous person (Virgil, an ancient Roman poet, used the expression "a snake in the grass" (*Latet anguis in herba*) in 37 BCE in his book *Eclogues* (sometimes called the Bucolics). That is the first known use.

Snake oil salesman—A con artist selling a phony remedy.

Squirrel away—Hide for a later time.

Squirrely—A way of acting that is a bit anxious and unpredictable; moving a lot in a way that might not make sense, raises suspicions.

Wet as a drowned rat—Soaking wet.

Animal Outcast Picture Books

Badgers, opossums, and raccoons may be animals some people love to hate, but kids sure seem to love gentle bedtime stories featuring anthropomorphic versions of these trash animals. Here is a curated list of picture book recommendations featuring some of our favorite outsider animals (often snuggly warm inside).

"...look like the innocent flower,
But be the serpent under't."
Lady Macbeth, *Macbeth*, Act I, Scene V

- *Bedtime for Frances* by Russell Hoban, with illustrations by Garth Williams (1995)
  Frances is a badger who has many requests before she can go to sleep.

- *Oswald the Almost Famous Opossum* by Sara Katherine Pascoe (2016)
  Oswald befriends a human named Joey and goes on many adventures in pursuit of stardom.

- *Polly the Possum* by Tessie Ledesma (2023)
  Polly learns to celebrate what makes her unique.

- *But Not Stanleigh* by George Cloven and Barbara A. Steiner (1986)
  An exploration in photos of a real-life raccoon's morning adventures.

- *Brand-new Pencils, Brand-new Books* by Diane DeGroat (2007)
  Part of the "Gilbert and Friends" series that celebrates the colorful world of this friendly, furry first-grader.

- *The Young Teacher and the Great Serpent* by Irene Vasco (2023)
  Indigenous students in a small village in the Amazon rainforest are entranced by the teacher's books and inspired to tell their teacher a local serpent legend.

- *Rock Paper Incisors: A Skunk and Badger Story* by Amy Timberlake (2025)
  Things get complicated for two roommates when they bring two rat babies into their care.
- *Don't Let the Pigeon Drive the Bus!* by Mo Willems (2005)
  Part of the "Pigeon" series, this is a funny tale about a pushy pigeon.
- *The Girl Who Wore Snakes* by Angela Johnson (1993)
  A girl named Ali is drawn to snakes—and maybe she isn't the only one.

Let's not forget the famous friends from *The Wind in the Willows* by British writer Kenneth Grahame. The author began imagining Mole, Rat, Toad, and Badger in the bedtime stories he created for his son. The book kicks off when Mole tires of his spring-cleaning tasks and heads instead to the river. American president Theodore Roosevelt was a fan of this charmingly illustrated and kind-hearted book, and various stage and film adaptations followed.

"'Oh, Badger,' cried the Rat, 'let us in, please. It's me, Rat, and my friend Mole, and we've lost our way in the snow.'

'What, Ratty, my dear little man!' exclaimed the Badger, in quite a different voice. 'Come along in, both of you, at once. Why, you must be perished. Well I never! Lost in the snow! And in the Wild Wood, too, and at this time of night! But come in with you.'"

—*The Wind in the Willows* by Kenneth Grahame (1908)

Street Rats

The rat is a favorite figure for anonymous British street artist Banksy, presented with changing meanings that offer comment on life in cities. Banksy says of the rat: "They exist without permission. They are hated, hunted, and persecuted. They live in quiet desperation amongst the filth. And yet they are capable of bringing entire civilizations to their knees. If you are dirty, insignificant, and unloved, then rats are the ultimate role model."

Songs Inspired by Trash Animals

"Black Crow Blues" by Bob Dylan
"Rocky Raccoon" by The Beatles
"Eager Beaver" by Stan Kenton
"Andy's Chest" by Lou Reed
"Smell of Petroleum" by The Pogues
"The Badger Song" by The Dead Milkmen
"Dead Skunk" by Loudon Wainwright III
"The Little Red Fox" by Kay Kyser
"*Les deux pigeons*" by Charles Aznavour
"Poisoning Pigeons in the Park" by Tom Lehrer
"Rats" by Pearl Jam
"Cold Hearted Snake" by Paula Abdul
"I Love Trash" by Oscar the Grouch (Jeff Moss)
"I'm a Raccoon" by The Briefs
"Raccoon's Got a Bushy Tail" by Pete Seeger
"Playing Possum" by George Jones
"Sally's Pigeons" by Cyndi Lauper and
Mary Chapin Carpenter
"Crows" by The Gothic Archies

SALLY'S PIGEONS

In 2022, when the United States Supreme Court overturned Roe v. Wade, Cyndi Lauper recorded a new version of her song "Sally's Pigeons." The song, co-written with Mary Chapin Carpenter for the 1993 album *Hat Full of Stars*, was a tribute to Lauper's childhood friend who died after a back-alley abortion that took place before terminations were legalized on a national level in 1973. The song describes the memory of watching pigeons "dive and soar" when the singer and her late friend were young children playing imaginary games.

Cinematic Trash Animals

Fans of Disney's 2007 hit *Enchanted* might remember the scene when trash animals bring a touch of gritty urban reality to the Manhattan apartment where the princess Giselle (played by Amy Adams) sings the "Happy Working Song." Rats scrub the toilet, pigeons help put away the plates (or try, the sound of a shattering plate wakes the sleeping six-year-old), and cockroaches even join in the singing. The amusing scene satirizes iconic Disney classics, such as "A Dream is a Wish Your Heart Makes," where birds and mice help Cinderella get ready in the morning, or Snow White's "With a Smile and a Song," where she's cheered up by a choir of adorable woodland animals. (Look closely—you'll spot raccoons and squirrels among them!) Who says the ensemble can't be assembled from the trash?

Besides teaching us that irreverent *SNL* cast members can star in one of the most beloved Christmas movies of all time, *Elf* (2003) taught us how not to approach animals in the wild. Buddy the Elf (Will Ferrell) is making his epic journey from the North Pole to New York City, when he comes across a raccoon and asks its name. The raccoon warns him not to come closer, standing on its hind legs and hissing. Buddy the Elf doesn't get the hint and asks, "Does someone need a hug?" That's when the raccoon goes in for the attack.

• • •

The Lost Weekend was a 1945 film noir directed by Billy Wilder about an alcoholic on a drinking spree, played by Ray Milland. In one scene, the main character hallucinates a bat—by many accounts, one of this Oscar-winning film's most memorable sequences.

Thousands of birds flew across the screen for Alfred Hitchcock's iconic 1963 film *The Birds*, starring Tippi Hedren, including gulls, ravens, sparrows, and crows.

The movie was partly based on a 1952 short story by Daphne du Maurier, as well as a real-life incident where poisoned birds went on the attack in Capitola, a town on the California coast a few hours south of Bodega Bay where the movie takes place. (Hitchcock supplemented the real birds with mechanical versions to add to the ominous feel.)

"... Red Fox darted indignantly up a lane, through a garden, and out across the back fields, still keeping his face toward those dark shapes of mountain towering against the western sky. In a very few minutes the clamour of the village curs was left behind. At last he crossed a noisy, shallow brook; and then the ground began to rise. Wild underbrush was all about him, and ancient trees; and soon he was climbing among rocks more harsh and hugely tumbled than those of his native Ringwaak. Once only he stopped—having heard some tiny squeaks among the tree-roots—long enough to catch a woodmouse, which eased his long hunger. Then he pressed on, ever climbing; till, in the first gray-saffron transparency of dawn, he came out upon a jutting cape of rock, and found himself in a wilderness to his heart's desire, a rugged turbulence of hills and ravines where the pack and the scarlet hunters could not come."

—*Red Fox* by Sir Charles G.D. Roberts (1905)

RUNWAY PIGEON

Who would guess a pigeon would make it to the world of luxury fashion? Northern Irish fashion designer Jonathan Anderson spotted the haute-couture possibilities in the ubiquitous city bird. His pigeon clutch goes for $890. The designer presented the bag in his fall 2022 collection, and it made its way to Sarah Jessica Parker on the set of *And Just Like That* . . . (Season 2).

• • •

A snake gets a starring role in Italian sculptor and painter Michelangelo's *The Fall of Man* (1510), painted on the ceiling of the Sistine Chapel. The painting, also called *The Fall and Expulsion from Garden of Eden; Adam and Eve*, depicts the story of Adam and Eve from *Genesis*. In one scene the fresco painting shows Adam and Eve being tempted to eat from the forbidden Tree of Knowledge (a fig tree) and then being cast out from the garden.

DUST OF SNOW

By Robert Frost (1923)

The way a crow
Shook down on me
The dust of snow
From a hemlock tree

Has given my heart
A change of mood
And saved some part

Of a day I had rued.

PLANET PROTECTORS

Could it be that so-called trash animals actually help us keep our planet clean? Just for starters, raccoons and beavers help boost pollinator populations and badgers protect wildlife. Read on to find out more about what these bandits and their band of merry misfits do to help the Earth.

Beavers

Beavers may be the champion planet protector among this group of trash animals. North America's largest rodent is known as a keystone species, which means they have an outsize impact on the environment. Most people probably associate beavers with dam-building, but many may not have stopped to think about the actual purpose of those dams. Beavers block water flow to create deep pools, where they build their shelter, or "lodge." They then create canals or tunnels, which they use to enter and exit their lodges through the water.

It turns out that the dams help more than just the beavers, offering a safe habitat for myriad creatures and ameliorating both flooding and soil erosion, for a start. The dams can create additional wetlands, stimulating the growth of plants and establishing a habitat where many species prosper. The wetlands are important in the fight against wildfires and can also offer protection for wildlife during fires. Wetlands also take in greenhouse gas. Finally, water quality is improved as nutrients collect in the sheltered ponds and provide a kind of water-filtering process.

Raccoons

Pollinators are essential to life on Earth, contributing to cleaner air, healthier water and soils, and the ability to grow most of our crops. The loss of pollinators is therefore a critical sustainability issue, and raccoons help us address it by eating one of the bees' main enemies—wasps. They also help reduce the rodent population and clean up dead animals. Finally, by eating fruits and nuts they help to spread seeds and boost plant growth.

Opossums

Like raccoons, opossums do their part to help minimize rodent overpopulation and clean up carrion. Slugs and snails get swept up by these nocturnal scavengers as well. Opossums also pollinate a mysterious plant called *Scybalium fungiforme*. The fungus-like plant is found in Brazil, where it is called Cogumelo-de-caboclo.

Bats

Like other trash animals, bats feed on insects, and some also spread seeds. Certain bat species are pollinators as well. The Mexican long-nosed bat and the Lesser long-nosed bat are both important pollinators for agave plants that grow in semi-arid and arid regions. Agave syrup (or nectar) comes from the sap of the agave plant, which is endangered by climate change, over-production, and other forces.

Bats are a major point of attraction at several U.S. National Parks, including Carlsbad Caverns National Park, Great Basin National Park, and Saguaro National Park. At Carlsbad Caverns, for example, visitors enjoy the daily bat flight, when Brazilian free-tailed bats swoop out of the caverns near sundown looking for dinner. Bats help educate tourists about the parks' ecosystems, amplify seed dispersal by eating fruits, and bring nutrients into caves that support a diverse group of organisms. There are over 45 different species of bats throughout the parks.

Snakes

Like other animals called pests, snakes help balance the ecosystem by keeping mice populations under control. Timber rattlesnakes eat rodents that host the ticks that transmit Lyme disease. Scientists also rely on venom from snakes such as the pit vipers that are native to North America to create antivenom treatments, as well as other types of medicine. The black mamba snake from Africa has one of the deadliest bites on the planet—it's 100 percent fatal if not treated. Yet the venom has shown great promise in the creation of a new painkiller.

Squirrels

Most people know that squirrels like to bury acorns and nuts in the ground, but you might not think about what happens next. Ideally for the squirrels, they find the food they squirreled away, but just as often they forget where they hid it. That means squirrels end up planting seeds that grow into new trees. In this way, they help with the regeneration of forests and enhance biodiversity. It turns out that nuts from certain trees, including walnut and hickory, often would not flourish where they land. Without squirrels picking up the seeds and burying them in another location, most of these trees would not grow.

Given that forests are carbon sinks—taking in more carbon than they release—squirrels contribute to our efforts to battle climate change by supporting forest growth.

Red Foxes

Red foxes establish homes that other animals, such as rabbits and badgers, can also use. Creating their dens may also contribute to soil aeration. Like other "nuisance" animals, the red fox helps control rodent populations. As predators of mice—vectors for Lyme disease— red foxes likely play a role in limiting Lyme disease infection in humans. Scientists speculate that mice may stay hidden when red foxes are present, meaning fewer ticks contract Lyme and other tick-borne diseases through biting infected mice. Fewer infected ticks means fewer incidents of disease transmission to humans. A bit of a complicated web, but a reminder that we are indeed part of a rather complex ecosystem of organisms that are dependent on each other.

Crows

Though farmers have long tried to keep them away—even creating scarecrows as a dedicated decoy to scare them off—crows can actually help boost agriculture output by feeding on pests, such as grubs and caterpillars, that would otherwise harm crops. Consuming carrion also helps cut down on insect infestation, and crows spread pollen as well, by transferring it between flowers, where it sticks to their bills and feathers. In China, scientists have documented crows' contribution to seed dispersal of an endangered tree called the Chinese yew (*Taxus chinensis*).

Badgers

Particularly in Europe, badgers support biodiversity and improve soil health with their digging and foraging. They also help break down plant material and support the stabilization of their environment with the dens they build. These dens—called setts—are complex arrangements of tunnels and "rooms," or chambers that offer protection to other wildlife, such as rabbits, weasels, and foxes, as well as organisms such as plants and fungi. Given all the ways they boost biodiversity, badgers are highly valued ecosystem engineers (organisms that alter their environment in a dramatic and lasting way). Furthermore, they are often appealing to children because of their cute, striped faces and digging superpower. For this reason, badgers make a popular subject for nature education, providing a portal to further environmental studies for the next generation.

Pigeons

Like other trash animals, pigeons do their part in protecting the planet by eating insects and garbage. They also help spread seeds and pollen. Plus, pigeons have played a pivotal role in our understanding of the natural world. Much of what we know about natural selection comes from Charles Darwin's studies of pigeons. Like many others in Victorian England, Darwin bred and cross-bred pigeons; they played a major role in his seminal 1859 book on evolution, *On the Origin of Species*. What's more, they played a starring role in his lesser-known, but nonetheless groundbreaking, 1868 book *The Variation of Animals and Plants Under Domestication*. Whenever we stop to admire the stunning diversity of life on Earth, we can thank pigeons for the contribution they made to our understanding of it. Finally, pigeons—in their urban ubiquity—are well-positioned to help humans learn to embrace our coexistence with other species, even ones who steal our picnic food when we're not looking ...

Skunks

By eating pests that plague farms and gardens, skunks help farmers and anyone growing crops or flowers. The role of skunks may be a bit humbler than that of squirrels planting trees and beavers helping protect wildlife from wildfire, but it remains a help nonetheless. Still not sold? Skunks also contribute by eating cockroaches, spiders, rodents, and snakes.

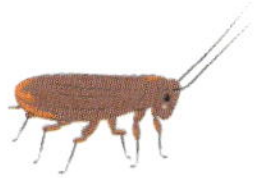

Rats

Climate change is boosting the rat population—a new study published in *Science Advances* shows increasing rat infestation in warming areas, including Washington, D.C., San Francisco, Toronto, New York City, and Amsterdam. It's hard to make a strong case for rats helping the Earth, but as the planet heats up and rats become more abundant, perhaps more people will get on board to start making more Earth-friendly choices (walk whenever possible and eat less meat are two great ways to start), if only to avoid a rat run-in! No one wants to be a rat on a sinking ship.

Protecting Trash (and other types of) Animals from Trash

We would be remiss in a book about trash animals not to mention how all animals are harmed by the trash we generate. You may remember being told to cut six-pack plastic rings so that they would not get caught around the mouth of dolphins and other sea creatures. The plastic pollution in our oceans, of course, affects countless animals—both the big pieces that might strangle or choke them, and the microplastics that get into their brains, just like they get into ours. It's not hard to find devastating images of all kinds of animals—on land as well—caught in our plastic bags or holding plastic debris in their mouths. Here are a few small things you can do:

- Put lids back on jars and bottles before discarding.
- Buy from companies that don't use excessive packaging.
- Use an animal-proof container for your trash and recycling.
- Compost to keep food waste out of landfills and make your trash less attractive to wildlife.
- Remember your reusable water bottle.
- And yes, you may as well snip those six-pack plastic rings.

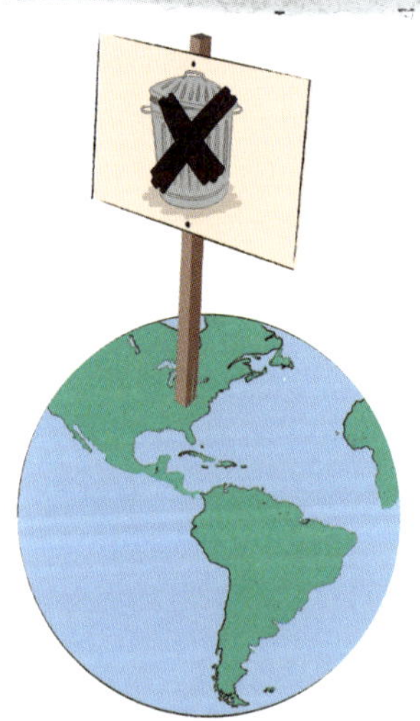

TRASH SPIRIT ANIMAL QUIZ

You may have a spirit animal, but the question of the moment is, do you have a *trash spirit animal?* Given the 3.5 million tons of solid rubbish that Earthlings produce daily, we might all just need one to guide us in the years to come. But maybe the future's not as bleak as it seems. After all, one person's trash is another's ________ (hint: rhymes with "pleasure"). Answer the following questions to find out which trash animal might be your spirit guide.

1. **A friend cancels dinner, and suddenly you have a free Friday evening stretching out ahead of you. Do you ...**

   a) Slightly panic and make a new plan immediately.

   b) Relish the time for a craft night home alone.

   c) Sleep.

   d) Let the friend know you're not thrilled to be suddenly dumped, even though you enjoy your own company.

   e) Find something nearby to nibble on while you plot your next step.

2. **You see a painting left out by the trash bins. Someone is clearly getting rid of it, but you happen to love the artwork. Do you ...**

   a) Look around and make sure it's definitely trash, so no one mistakes you for a bandit.

   b) Take it home to repurpose into a room divider in your studio.

c) Get inspired to start painting as a hobby.

d) Find a nice place to hang it in your den.

e) Wonder if you're part of an experiment.

3. **What do you see in this image? Don't think too much about it, just pick the first answer that occurs to you.**

   a) Something to explore.

   b) Your childhood home.

   c) The Garden of Eden.

   d) Cabbage.

   e) Political protest art.

4. **During what part of the day do you feel most productive?**

   a) First thing in the morning when I'm still in a partial dream-state.

   b) Later on, after I've had a chance to exercise, eat breakfast, check the news, and get through my emails.

   c) Twilight.

d) All my beastie besties know I come alive at night.

e) Whenever the neighborhood cats are asleep.

5. **On vacation in a new city overseas would you rather ...**

   a) Hit all the top attractions, stopping only for photo opps.

   b) Explore one neighborhood in detail, popping into little shops, chatting with locals, having a leisurely picnic by the river with cheese and wine that are favorites of the region.

   c) Bask in the sun.

   d) Happily stay in a shed somewhere, making sure it's close to water.

   e) Explore the underground tunnels.

6. **You're entering the subway after an afternoon of ice skating. As you're walking down the stairs, you become aware of a strange burning smell. Everyone in the station is acting like things are normal. They're going through the turnstile and getting on the train, even though a clear smoke is hanging in the air. Do you ...**

   a) Charge ahead boldly with your trip as if everything is normal, hopping on the train and dreaming of the beach.

   b) Turn around and fly home.

   c) Find the closest sheltered spot you can.

   d) Make yourself look as threatening as possible.

   e) Think back to the last time something like this happened and find the fastest way to safety, even if you have to go through a maze to get there.

7. At a bar on a Saturday night, which one sounds most like you?

a) Start with a bite to eat, but before actually consuming anything you take time to examine it, possibly even dunking it into your Dark n' Stormy, despite the sideways glances from the people sitting next to you.

b) Strut and dance around a bit, showing off the fabulous cape you found at a thrift store, and perhaps even crooning along with Frank Sinatra.

c) There's no time like the present for a total reinvention. If you're usually a wallflower, tonight you're in the center of the dance floor, letting loose for "Shake, Rattle, and Roll." If you spend most nights sipping Viper hard seltzer, today you're splashing down a Manhattan. If you're the social butterfly most nights, tonight you'll hang back and watch the mosh pit from afar.

d) Cannabis is more your speed than alcohol, so you're likely in a city where it's legal, sniffing out a dispensary.

e) Gently turning down your date's thoughtful but misguided gesture of ordering a cheese board and reaching for a bowl of nuts instead.

8. Which of the following behaviors would you be most likely to engage in?

a) Steal.

b) Fall for a scam.

c) Back-stab someone.

d) Take revenge.

e) Snitch.

9. Which superhero do you most resemble?

a) Ms. Marvel.

b) Supergirl.

c) Black Panther.

d) Stinkor.

e) Rat-Man.

10. What book would you most like to read?

a) *Brave New World* by Aldous Huxley.

b) *Lonesome Dove* by Larry McMurtry.

c) *Across the River and into the Trees* by Ernest Hemingway.

d) *The Outsiders* by S.E. Hinton.

e) *We Have Always Lived in the Castle* by Shirley Jackson.

Mostly As—Raccoon

You like to socialize with others, and you're especially active at night. You take to water as a natural swimmer, and climbing activities appeal to you as well. You're open-minded when it comes to food, enjoying a wide range of flavors, and you're unafraid of confrontation, even when you're caught doing something wrong. Your fearlessness can be empowering, but don't let a lack of fear block you from the chance to learn from your mistakes. You're curious, mischievous, and drawn to new paths of discovery. Adaptability generally serves you well, but remember, you don't have to change yourself to fit other people's expectations. Take off your mask every once in a while and find out who you are without it.

Mostly Bs—Pigeon

You're more intelligent than most people give you credit for, with an internal sense of direction that the inventors of GPS could only dream of. You're loyal to your mate, and though you have the capacity to soar way above the crowd, you tend to be happy hanging around your flock. Be aware of those who need more quiet and personal space than you do. If you find others getting annoyed by your presence, ask yourself if it's your problem or theirs: Did you inadvertently cross an important boundary? Keep in mind that others won't always see it, but you have a lot to offer. You don't feel the need to show off, but nonetheless, your colors shine. You know who you are, and, equally as important, you know how to find your way home.

Mostly Cs—Snake

You often scare people, maybe because you move through spaces with an ease that others find unnerving. It could also be your tireless ability to reinvent yourself, shedding your skin, and perhaps signaling to others that they should pursue their own personal transformation. You're solitary, and you don't have much of a voice, but you're quick-witted, sensitive, intuitive, and some might say cunning. You might even gain a reputation for deception, but you'll only bite in self-defense. You don't ask for a lot, and you're always aware of your surroundings. Continue seeking out social bonds that are supportive, but learn to accept that you're not everyone's cup of tea. Healing and renewal are your birthrights, and you'll continue slithering on your merry way.

Mostly Ds—Skunk

Even though you don't have the best reputation, some try to make you into their pet. That might not be the best idea—you're a creature of the night and you tend to keep to yourself. And it's no wonder: attempts to simply defend yourself often end up earning you cruel nicknames. You know you're not aggressive, but you are powerful, and power always threatens the weak. You like to dig below the surface and explore new spaces, but before you do either, make sure you're not intruding. Wear your stripes proudly and don't wander too far from home—you may not find your way back.

Mostly Es—Rat

Some people think you're adorable; others are paralyzed in terror at the sight of you. The wide range of reactions should be enough to tell you not to put too much stake in what others think. You're social and tend to be active at night. You'll have an easy time with modern plant-based diets, preferring nuts, fruits, and grains, despite your reputation as a cheese-lover. You have an expressive face and you're on the skittish side, but the shakiness is not entirely unfounded—you actually do have quite a few enemies, and others like to use you as a guinea pig. Try not to become the subject of others' experiments. Instead, enjoy the little time you have, make use of your organizational abilities, your athletic skills, on both land and water, and your highly developed sense of empathy.

INSPIRATION AND ADDITIONAL RESOURCES

Further reading

SITES

Save the Snakes
https://savethesnakes.org/why-snakes/

Awesome Possumz
www.awesomepossumz.com/

Space for Badgers
www.badgertrust.org.uk/space-for-badgers

Mainely Rat Rescue
https://mainelyratrescue.org/rattieblog2/

Animals you love to hate
www.reconnectwithnature.org/news-events/big-features/the-facts-about-the-animals-you-love-to-hate/

Forget everything you think you know about pigeons
www.nationalgeographic.com/animals/article/pigeons-diversity-doves-photographs

BOOKS

In Defense of the World's Most Despised Species: Why We Love Some Species but Hate Most, and Why It Matters by Ernest Small. Boca Raton, FL: CRC Press, 2023.

Raccoon by Daniel Heath Justice. Chicago: University of Chicago Press, 2021.

Some We Love, Some We Hate, Some We Eat: Why It's So Hard to Think Straight About Animals by Hal Herzog. New York: Harper Perennial, 2011.

Trash Animals: How We Live with Nature's Filthy, Feral, Invasive, and Unwanted Species by Kelsi Nagi and Phillip David Johnson II. Minnesota: University of Minnesota Press, 201.

PODCASTS

Science In The City: Cylita Guy Talks Chasing Bats And Tracking Rats. February 3, 2022. Short Wave, NPR.

Red Fox. Relax with Animal Facts: A Podcast. 10/7/2022. Episode 121. 23 minutes hosted by Stefan Wolfe.

O Possum! My Possum! November 23, 2022. Outside/In: A show where curiosity and the natural world collide. https://outsideinradio.org/shows/o-possum-my-possum

Trash Animal Inspiration

A blind baby opossum was about three months old when she was found by Karen Brace, a wildlife rehabber on Eva Drive in Port Royal, Virginia, U.S.A. Brace was able to get a license to continue to care for the orphaned opossum she named Eva, and even made Eva the ambassador at her Awesome Possumz organization (www.awesomepossumz.com).

• • •

In China during the fifth century BCE, no one would have mistaken snakes and rats for trash animals. They are two of the twelve Zodiac signs that were made official centuries later, during the Han Dynasty. The Year of the Snake in the Chinese Zodiac is 2025 (along with 1929, 1941, 1953, 1965, 1977, 1989, 2001, and 2013). The snake (*she*) has a multiplicity of meanings in Chinese culture, including rebirth and good luck. They are also thought of as little dragons.

YEAR OF THE SNAKE

Greek philosopher Antisthenes (a student of Socrates) may have founded the Cynic school of philosophy, but he had a positive thought about the bird often associated with bad luck:

"It is better to fall among crows than flatterers; for those devour only the dead—these the living."

• • •

In the 1950s at Harvard University, American biologist Dr. Curt Richter conducted an upsetting study (sometimes called the drowning rats experiment) that showed rats who had hope were able to swim for longer than those who didn't. The study has had many implications on how hope can increase resilience.

Celebrating Trash Animals Throughout the Year

January 21 – National Squirrel Appreciation Day
April 4 – World Rat Day
April 7 – International Beaver Day
April 17 – International Bat Appreciation Day
April 27 – International Crow and Raven Appreciation Day
June 13 – Pigeon Appreciation Day
June 14 – National Skunk Day
July 16 – World Snake Day
September 17 – National Fox Day
October 1 – International Raccoon Appreciation Day
October 6 – National Badger Day
October 18 – National Opossum Day

Photographer Dick Van Duijn, based in Holland, created a "Squirrel Series"—incredibly popular photographs of a squirrel smelling different flowers. (The daisy was the favorite.) The viral sensation shots were taken in Vienna, Austria. Van Duijn hopes his work will inspire people to spend more time in nature.

Beavers Wetlands & Wildlife established International Beaver Day in 2009 on the birthday of conservationist Dorothy Richards (1894–1985), A.K.A. "Beaver Woman," who devoted herself to the study of beavers and wrote *Beaversprite: My Years Building an Animal Sanctuary*, published in 1977.

If you're lucky enough to visit the Fire Island National Seashore on Long Island in New York State, U.S.A., look out for the sight of the abundant red fox enjoying the park, home to more than 30 species of mammals. In the Navajo language, the red fox is called *Máii iiłtsoí* (orange-colored coyote), and the Navajo Nation believes this cunning animal has healing powers. Wildlife biologist Sarah Karpanty, professor in the Department of Fish and Wildlife Conservation at Virginia Tech, has been studying red fox ecology on Fire Island. For the sake of the animals (and us), she advises visitors not to feed the foxes.

The United States Fish and Wildlife Service listed the subspecies Sierra Nevada red fox (*Vulpes vulpes necator*) on their endangered list in 2021. Loss of their snowy habitat due to climate change is one factor that has threatened their survival. As of that year, there were only estimated to be 39 of these foxes left. Groups like Defenders of Wildlife and WildEarth Guardians, however, are bringing attention to the mountain-roaming fox and the hobbies like snowmobiling that harm them, with the hopes of building their numbers back up.

A retirement home in the suburbs of Philadelphia brings in an emotional support skunk named Meadows to provide comfort to the senior citizens who live there.

Trash animals that symbolize good luck according to some belief systems:

Snake
Beaver
Crow
Rat
Badger
Bat
Fox
and sometimes opossum

Epilogue: Left Out of the Out Crowd

It wasn't easy narrowing down the list of animal misfits to come up with the twelve we ended up including in this book. Skunks had to be part of the group, of course, and probably pigeons, squirrels, rats, and raccoons. Beavers alter the environment quite a bit but mind their own business. Still, like they do for snakes and bats, people call Pest Control to deal with beavers on their property. Badgers and opossums are high on the cute-quotient and tend not to be aggressive, but people with yards could find them a nuisance. Same with foxes. And crows have had a bit of a bad reputation for eons.

Still, there were others we tossed around, like carp and coyote, bear, bluejay, or bobcat. Depending on where we live, we all likely have different takes on which animals are first of all enough of a nuisance to be shooed away by many, but with enough charming qualities to be redeemed in a book like this one. In this section, we'll take a look at two more that we could have included: the snot otter and the coyote.

SNOT OTTER

(Cryptobranchus alleganiensis alleganiensis)

First up, the Eastern hellbender salamander (A.K.A. the snot otter). This unappealing salamander, with an equally unappealing nickname, has suffered an immense loss of habitat due to a range of factors, including pollution, dam projects, and climate change. While the Ozark hellbender is listed as endangered, the U.S. Fish and Wildlife Service has not yet labeled the Eastern version as endangered, despite dwindling numbers.

Fortunately, the meandering salamander has its champions. The International Union for Conservation of Nature lists the creature as near-threatened. In

September 2024, the Center for Biological Diversity in Somerset, Kentucky, sent a 40-plus-page letter arguing for the protection of the hellbender, which they pointed out has been around since the time of Pangea before the continents split apart. The letter, called "RE: The Hellbender Warrants Protection under the Endangered Species Act," references a *National Geographic* article from the 1970s that called the creature "repulsive" and a "wrinkled horror," but notes that today the creature has status as "a charismatic poster child for clean rivers."

In April of 2019, the snot otter became Pennsylvania's official state amphibian. The unlikely mascot is harmless, despite rumors to the contrary, and goes by many creative names, but champions of the nocturnal vertebrate focused on a single aspect to make their case: Its value as a marker of clean water.

High school students on the Chesapeake Bay Foundation's leadership council drew attention to the stream-loving hellbender when their study of water protection led them to discover the salamanders' presence was an accurate predictor of clean water.

Since 1990, their population has declined significantly, an indicator that Pennsylvania needs to

NICKNAMES:

Snot otter
Spotted water gecko
Lasagna lizard
Devil dog
Mud devil
Old lasagna sides
Grampus
Allegheny alligator

prioritize water protection. One hundred and ninety-one members of the state's house of representatives voted to coronate the wrinkly creature as the official state amphibian. (Six representatives voted against.) On April 23, Governor Tom Wolf signed the bill into law. The Pennsylvania Capital-Star called the move a "call to arms for environmental action."

With a range extending from the bottom of New York state to the top of Georgia, the hellbenders are the country's only giant salamander. (The world's largest giants live in China and Japan.) Choosing a state amphibian is a relatively recent phenomenon. In 1985, New Hampshire chose the red-spotted newt; a year later, Arizona picked the Arizona tree frog, and other states began to follow suit. The hellbender may be the least conventionally attractive pick. Reporting in *The Washington Post*, Sarah Kaplan described its look "as though someone yanked out a giant's esophagus, gave it legs and taught it to swim." According to the Missouri Department of Conservation, the creature's official name comes from an unsettling thought it sparked in the minds of early American settlers—the "horrible tortures of the infernal regions." This "creature from hell where it's bent on returning" was given the name that's stayed. But the hellbender may just end up helping humans bend away from devastating changes to our environment.

COYOTE

(Canis latrans)

Now let's move on to the coyote, often called the "most hated" animal in the United States. Like the fox, they're members of the dog family *Canidae* and are found in packs throughout North America. Their scientific name means "barking dog" in Latin, and they're known for the sound of their group howls at night. Coyotes can run up to 40 miles an hour (a raccoon can run up to 15, a red fox up to 31, badgers, surprisingly, can reach 19).

An important symbolic animal in Native American mythology, coyotes have endured for at least a million years. As their natural predators, such as the mountain lion, declined, they spread east and their population paradoxically surges the more they are hunted. One reason for this is that access to more nutrition among a smaller group leads to stronger offspring. Another is that they have a kind of built-in population control where the size of their litters expands to counteract perceived low numbers. How do they count? They listen for the response to their howls. If they don't receive a response, they start giving birth to higher numbers of pups.

Lewis and Clark, in their discovery expedition across the U.S., wrote about their encounters with coyote in 1804 in what is now South Dakota. They dubbed the animal prairie wolf; coyote comes from the name given by the Aztecs. Coyotes have taken various hits to their reputation, from Mark Twain to the Bureau of Biological Survey (a government agency) that poisoned close to 6.5 million coyotes in the mid-twentieth century. Although the poisoning mostly stopped in the 1970s, roughly half a million coyotes are still killed yearly. They tend to fare well in cities now, but it's always best not to feed them. Acclimating them to humans will put them in danger of being euthanized. It's better to let them keep to their elusive nature.

NICKNAMES:

Little wolf
American jackal
Prairie wolf
Brush wolf

PIGEON APOLOGIA

Humans began domesticating pigeons thousands of years ago, probably as a food source and later to take advantage of the birds' "homing instinct." Pigeons likely helped the people of Mesopotamia deliver messages. They appear in the ancient Sumerian poem "Epic of Gilgamesh" written on tablets 4,000 years ago. Even earlier, the Bible recounts the story of Noah employing doves (believed to be homing pigeons) to ascertain the state of the flood waters. Ancient Greeks conveyed news of victory in battle via carrier pigeons, and later Julius Caesar relied on pigeons for communication. Through World War II, pigeons were revered for their navigational powers, but technology moved fast, and we now have more efficient methods to communicate. Still, we might do well to remember that we were the ones who brought these urban castoffs into our lives the next time we try to cast them out of our picnic. The urban "pests" that we ostracize are feral descendants of our once domesticated pets. Their ancestors were wild rock doves who spent their days darting into caves and perched on cliffs overlooking the ocean.

CONCLUSION

Many of us think of animals like squirrels, pigeons, and crows as a nuisance to shoo out of the way as we hurry about our day. We might rarely stop to think about the fact that squirrels help plant trees, pigeons won awards in World War II, and crows might understand the concept of zero, even though it took humans centuries. Hopefully this book has given you some insight into how much there is to admire about the animals we so often think of as pests to be controlled rather than species to appreciate.

Perhaps when you next encounter an animal you typically dismiss, you can take time to observe it from a safe distance. It's quite remarkable, for instance, how squirrels use their hands to eat, in a dainty act of etiquette that our pampered house pets might envy if they had any table manners themselves. We don't love the sound of a crow cawing like we do the call of a common loon, but perhaps we can appreciate the variety of vocalizations, and the sophistication of their communication, if we hear them "speak" to each other.

Whether animals are cute and amusing or a bit terrifying, intelligent or not, contributing to reforestation or simply climbing trees, trash animals, like all animals, are a vital part of our natural ecosystem. Their histories are fascinating, as are their representations in art and popular culture, and many do contribute to our wellbeing, even as we continually interfere with theirs. But perhaps we can recognize all their contributions and at the same time let them be part of the complex web of life we're lucky to be a part of as well. Some eat insects that bother us, others are eaten by animals we admire, like the mountain lion or the bald eagle, but whether through our backyards, our nutrient cycle, or our shared need to survive on a warming planet, perhaps the fundamental message these outsider animals give us is that we are all connected, and, no matter what the popular kids told us in the school cafeteria, we all belong here.

SELECT BIBLIOGRAPHY

Angier, Natalie. A Fast Life and Success That Starts in the Pouch, *New York Times*, June 13, 2011, www.nytimes.com/2011/06/14/science/14angier.html#:~:text=Embryonic%20opossums%20spend%20about%2012,the%20next%20couple%20of%20months.

"Badgers," The Zoological Society. Web Accessed May 14, 2025. https://www.zsl.org/what-we-do/species/badger

Badger Trust, Badger Trust launches new 'Space for Badgers' campaign, www.badgertrust.org.uk/post/badger-trust-launches-new-space-for-badgers-campaign

Bai, B., et al. Bulbuls and crows provide complementary seed dispersal for China's endangered trees. *Avian Res* 8, 31 (2017). https://doi.org/10.1186/s40657-017-0089-y

Bat Conservation International, Bats and Agave: A love story, www.batcon.org/batsandagave/

Bayern, A.M.P.v., Danel, S., Auersperg, A.M.I., et al. Compound tool construction by New Caledonian crows. *Sci Rep* 8, 15676 (2018). https://doi.org/10.1038/s41598-018-33458-z

Beavers are "ecosystem engineers" and fight climate change, too, *Wildlife & Wild Places*, March 30, 2023, https://environmentamerica.org/articles/beavers-are-ecosystem-engineers-and-fight-climate-change-too/#:~:text=Beavers%20help%20control%20water%20flow.&text=Dams%20physically%20store%20water%20on,place%20thanks%20to%20their%20dams.

Black Death 'spread by humans not rats', BBC News, January 15, 2018, www.bbc.com/news/science-environment-42690577

Brookshire, Bethany. Maybe dogs didn't need us at all to domesticate themselves, *National Geographic*, February 11, 2025, www.nationalgeographic.com/animals/article/math-model-dog-self-domestication

Capoccia, Stella, Boyle, Callie, Darnell, Tedd. Loved or loathed, feral pigeons as subjects in ecological and social research, *Journal of Urban Ecology*, Volume 4, Issue 1, 2018, juy024, https://doi.org/10.1093/jue/juy024

Carrington, Damian. "Humanity has wiped out 60% of animal populations since 1970, report finds." *Guardian*. May 29, 2018. Web Accessed May 14, 2025. https://www.theguardian.com/environment/2018/oct/30/humanity-wiped-out-animals-since-1970-major-report-finds

Ceballos, G., Ehrlich, P.R., Dirzo, R. "Biological annihilation via the ongoing sixth mass extinction signaled by vertebrate population losses and declines", *Proc. Natl. Acad. Sci. U.S.A.* 114 (30) E6089-E6096, https://doi.org/10.1073/pnas.1704949114 (2017).

Cibulski, L., et al. Familiarity with the experimenter influences the performance of Common ravens (*Corvus corax*) and Carrion crows (*Corvus corone corone*) in cognitive tasks. *Behav Processes*. 2014 Mar;103(100):129-37. doi: 10.1016/j.beproc.2013.11.013. Epub 2013 Dec 12. PMID: 24333226; PMCID: PMC4003535.

Davenport, Matt. Opossum Compounds Isolated to Help Make Antivenom, *Scientific American*, March 30, 2015, www.scientificamerican.com/article/opossum-compounds-isolated-to-help-make-antivenom/

The Editors of Encyclopaedia Britannica. "Badger". *Encyclopedia Britannica*, April 25 2025, https://www.britannica.com/animal/badger. Accessed May 14, 2025.

Every Day Home Advice Relating Chiefly to Household Management: With Hints Upon Houses, how to Construct and Preserve; Domestic Cookery in All Its Departments ... Together with Hints Upon Nearly Every Emergency that Arises During the Lifetime of Man, Woman Or Child. United Kingdom, G.W. Carleton & Company, 1883.

"European Badger Predators," Wildlife Online. Web Accessed May 13, 2025. https://www.wildlifeonline.me.uk/animals/article/european-badger-predators#:~:text=In%20Europe%20wolves%2C%20lynx%2C%20wolverines,of%20cubs%20and%20juvenile%20badgers.

Greenwood, Veronique. Deadly black mamba snake's venom could mean pain relief, *Time*, October 5, 2012, www.cnn.com/2012/10/05/health/snake-venom-pain-relief-time/index.html#:~:text=Hidden%20in%20the%20grim%20cocktail,unusual%20new%20source%20for%20painkillers.

Grooten, M. and Almond, R.E.A.(Eds). *WWF. 2018*. Living Planet Report – 2018: Aiming Higher. WWF, Gland, Switzerland.

Harmon, Amy. Lyme Disease's Worst Enemy? It Might Be Foxes, *New York Times*, August 2, 2017, www.nytimes.com/2017/08/02/science/ticks-lyme-disease-foxes-martens.html

Heimbuch, Jaymi. 8 Surprising Facts About Badgers, Treehugger, November 16, 2020, www.treehugger.com/surprising-badger-facts-4863670

Jackson, Laura. *Deep & Wild: On Mountains, Opossums & Finding Your Way in West Virginia*, Autumn House Press (2024)

Jones, Benji. Hate rats? Then you won't love this new study, *Vox*, February 3, 2025, www.vox.com/down-to-earth/397128/rats-new-york-city-dc-infestation-climate-change

Kircher, Jane. Opossums: Unsung Heroes in the Fight Against Tricks and Lyme Disease, NWF Blog, December 16, 2021, https://blog.nwf.org/2017/06/opossums-unsung-heroes-in-the-fight-against-ticks-and-lyme-disease/

Konstantinides, Anneta. "A photographer captured the exact moment a squirrel stopped to smell a daisy." *Business Insider*. https://www.businessinsider.com/photographer-captured-moment-squirrel-stopped-to-smell-daisy-2019-11

Macleish, Archibald. *Tower of Ivory*, New Haven: Yale University Press 1917

MacNeill, Kyle. How pigeons clawed back their cultural cachet, *Plaster*, October 2, 2024, https://plastermagazine.com/opinion/pigeon-art-cultural-trend/

Marinelli, Janet. How Preserving Agave Could Help Save an Endangered Bat, YaleEnvironment 360, February 1, 2022, https://e360.yale.edu/features/a-fine-balance-is-upended-among-agave-mexican-bats-and-humans

Mark, Joshua J., Pets in Colonial America, *World History Encyclopedia*, April 19, 2021, www.worldhistory.org/article/1728/pets-in-colonial-america/

Minta, S.C., Minta, K.A., Lott, D.F. (1992). Hunting Associations between Badgers (*Taxidea taxus*) and Coyotes (*Canis latrans*), *Journal of Mammalogy*, Vol. 73, No. 4, 814-820

Modlinska, K., Pisula, W. The Norway rat, from an obnoxious pest to a laboratory pet. Elife. 2020 Jan 17;9:e50651. doi: 10.7554/eLife.50651. PMID: 31948542; PMCID: PMC6968928.

National Archives, From Benjamin Franklin to Georgiana Shipley, September 26, 1772, https://founders.archives.gov/documents/Franklin/01-19-02-0202

National Park Service, Build a Beaver Dam, www.nps.gov/articles/buildabeaverdam.htm

National Wildlife Federation, About Ranger Rick, www.nwf.org/About-Us/History/About-Ranger-Rick

National Wildlife Federation, A Strange, Wondrous Beast of Our Backyards, www.nwf.org/Magazines/National-Wildlife/2003/American-Heritage-Opossum

Nature, Raccoon Facts, February 7, 2012, www.pbs.org/wnet/nature/raccoon-nation-raccoon-fact-sheet/7553/

New Hampshire Wildlife Coalition, Myths and Facts about Coyotes, https://nhwildlifecoalition.org/myths-and-facts-about-coyotes/

Nuwer, Rachel. Bats Act As Pest Control at Two Old Portuguese Libraries, *Smithsonian Magazine*, September 19, 2013, www.smithsonianmag.com/smart-news/bats-act-as-pest-control-at-two-old-portuguese-libraries-9950711/

Project Coyote, Protecting Wild Carnivores, Fostering thriving ecosystems, https://projectcoyote.org/

River Otter Ecology Project, Raccoon, https://riverotterecology.org/project/raccoon/#:~:text=The%20name%20%E2%80%9Draccoon%E2%80%9C%20came%20from,he%20scratches%20with%20his%20hands.

Rodrigues, Dania. The Italian Town that Welcomes Spring with Live Snakes, *Atlas Obscura*, May 5, 2023, www.atlasobscura.com/articles/snake-ritual-cocullo-italy

Save the Snakes, Why Snakes?, https://savethesnakes.org/why-snakes/

Serikawa, T. Colourful history of Japan's rat resources. *Nature* 429, 15 (2004), https://doi.org/10.1038/429015b

The History of "Squirrel", Merriam-Webster, www.merriam-webster.com/wordplay/the-history-of-squirrel

Trash Animals, Living on Earth, June 28, 2013, www.loe.org/shows/segments.html?programID=13-P13-00026&segmentID=5

U.S. Fish & Wildlife Service, Eastern Hellbender, www.fws.gov/species/eastern-hellbender-cryptobranchus-alleganiensis-alleganiensis

Watanabe, S., Sakamoto, J., Wakita, M. Pigeons' discrimination of paintings by Monet and Picasso. *J Exp Anal Behav.* 1995 Mar;63(2):165-74. doi: 10.1901/jeab.1995.63-165. PMID: 16812755; PMCID: PMC1334394.

Wertheimer, Tiffany. "Ronin the rat sets new landmine-sniffing record." BBC News, April 4, 2025. Web Accessed May 12, 2025. https://www.bbc.com/news/articles/c2ewxjjw842o

Winick, Stephen. A Possum Crisp and Brown: The Opossum and American Foodways, *Folklife Today*, August 15, 2019, https://blogs.loc.gov/folklife/2019/08/a-possum-crisp-and-brown-the-opossum-and-american-foodways/

Wildlife Rescue League, The Opossum: Our Marvelous Marsupial, The Social Loner, www.wildliferescueleague.org/animals/the-opossum-our-marvelous-marsupial-the-social-loner/

World Atlas, Why Are Crows Important To The Ecosystem?, www.worldatlas.com/articles/why-are-crows-important-to-the-ecosystem.html

Worrall, Simon. How the Most Hated Animal in America Outwitted Us All, *National Geographic*, August 7, 2016, www.nationalgeographic.com/animals/article/coyote-america-dan-flores-history-science.

INDEX

ABOUT THE AUTHOR AND ILLUSTRATOR

Rachel Federman is a writer, musician, and nonprofit consultant who has written over 20 books for adults and children, including *The Mindful Gardener* (Clarkson Potter, 2017) and *Test Your Dog's IQ* (HarperCollins, 2016). She started her career focused on the environment and is grateful to these rascal animals for their lessons in adaptation.

Clare Faulkner is a graphic designer and illustrator. She is the author and illustrator of *The Cat Lover's A to Z*, *The Dog Lover's A to Z*, and *The Fashion Classics* (2026) and is the illustrator of the bestselling "Animal philosophy" series by Jennifer McCartney, including *The Little Book of Sloth Philosophy*.

ACKNOWLEDGMENTS

Thanks always to my faithful friend and editor Caitlin Doyle. Glad you insisted we give these miscast outcasts their much-deserved day in the sun. I'm grateful as well to Clare Faulkner for capturing the mischief and fun of these animal outsiders, to Helena Caldon for her hawk-like copyedit and Rachel Malig for her thorough proofread. Thanks to the team at HarperCollins, e-Digital Design, Jacqui Caulton, and to the beloved baby Johnny One-note the Squirrel—and to the skunk who once slipped into our house late at night, mistaken for a cat, and left without fanfare threatened only with a raised chair.

Thank you to Lucy Vanderbilt, the original trash animal enthusiast. May books always be there to make dreams a reality! And to all those who feel misunderstood, jaded, and on the outside—we see you and you make our lives brighter, weirder, and more wonderful.